AUSTIN HEALEY
100/6 & 3000
All THE BIG 6~CYLINDER MODELS
John Wheatley

CONTENTS

A FOULIS Motoring Book

First published 1987

© **Haynes Publishing Group**

Published by:

Haynes Publishing Group,
Sparkford, Near Yeovil,
Somerset BA22 7JJ

Haynes Publications Inc.
861 Lawrence Drive, Newbury
Park, California 91320, USA

**British Library Cataloguing in
Publication Data**
Wheatley, John, 1929-
  Austin Healey 100/6 & 3000 : (all the
  big 6-cylinder models)—(Super profile)
  1. Austin-Healey automobile—History
  I. Title II. Series
  629.2'222   TL215.A92
  ISBN 0-85429-574-9

Library of Congress catalog card number
86-83181

Editor: Robert Iles
Series photographer: Andrew
Morland
Road tests: Courtesy of Autocar
Page layout: Peter Kay
Printed in England, by:
J.H. Haynes & Co. Ltd

Further titles in this series will be published at regular
intervals. For information on new titles please contact
your bookseller or write to the publisher.

FOREWORD

Mention the name "Austin-Healey" and the almost universal response will be, "You mean the 3000?" Although the original four cylinder cars and the smaller Sprites have a devoted following amongst enthusiasts for the marque, it is the 3000 and the other six cylinder derivatives which are the best known and remembered models from the whole product range. Doubtless much of the enduring impressions this model leaves in the minds of enthusiasts around the world is due to the outstanding Rally successes achieved in the early 1960s. In the hands of Makinen, Aaltonen, Pat Moss, the Morley brothers and other top drivers of the day the 3000 became a legend in its own lifetime. Not only was the car a formidable and seemingly indestructible performer, it was also a handsome machine which looked the part. Appearance did not flatter to deceive. Although in its final form, "The Big Healey" had clearly put on some bulk when compared with the original 100., it has also gained considerable muscle at the same time, to become the fastest and most comfortable of all Austin Healey models. Today, the 3000 Mk III is undeniably the most sought after of the volume produced Austin-Healeys and will surely continue to be so, since it is a car from an era never to return but which remains a completely practical vehicle capable of every day use.

I have always had the greatest affection for the Austin-Healey in all its derivative forms and although my first love will always remain with the 100, I have to confess a desire to own a two seat version of either the 3000 Mk I or Mk II models. These cars with their easy high performance and clean good looks have a very strong appeal and remain in the "Sports Car" category rather more than do the 3000 Mk IIa and Mk III models which despite their undoubted high performance have somewhat more of a "Sports Tourer" characteristic which is less to my personal taste. I feel sure that the reader will recognise the affection which I have for the Austin Healey marque, and for this reason it has given me much pleasure to write this book. In its preparation I have been fortunate to have the help of many equally enthusiastic people. My special thanks go to Anders Clausager of the British Motor Industry Heritage Trust who has had me over at Studley many times to carry out original research into all the Austin-Healey archive material held there. I also have to thank Austin Rover for the use of photographic archive material from both Longbridge and Cowley; *Motor* and *Autocar* magazines for permission to reproduce original contemporary road test material; Keith Clapham, Tony Matthews, Mike Powell, Tom Reece and Don Humphries for providing their cars for Andrew Morland to photograph. Andrew joins me in thanking the Chateau Impney at Droitwich for allowing us the use of the Hotel grounds for the photographic session. I am grateful to Dave Ramstad in the United States for his contribution to the Owner's View section for which Keith Clapham provided the U.K. viewpoint. Both Dave Ramstad and Roger Moment have provided photographs from their personal collections and Reid Trummel has advised on U.S. owners' Clubs. Don Humphries also very kindly provided detailed specification data on his unique 3000 Coupe.

The support and enthusiasm of all these people confirm my belief that the "Big Healey" continues to be an attractive, enjoyable and very practical sports car with an assured place in motoring history. Above all I must thank my family for their encouragement and help, especially my wife Heather for the preparation of the manuscript. She is as interested in Austin Healey cars as I am which makes me a very fortunate man!

John Wheatley

Austin Healey

HISTORY

The Donald Healey Motor Company was established at "The Cape" at Warwick in October 1946 and began car production with a Healey designed chassis fitted with Riley power units and bodies built by the Westland and Elliott specialist coach building companies. As bespoke vehicles, production volumes were low even by the standards of the day with a total of only 301 units being built until manufacture of these models ceased in early 1954. Whilst production of these two original definitive cars was running, several other models were introduced in parallel, and ran for various periods and volumes.

In October 1948 the Sportsmobile was launched, but was discontinued in 1950 with only 23 examples built. In the Summer of 1949 the first real Healey sports car, the Silverstone was announced. Built on the standard Healey chassis but with the Riley power unit repositioned slightly more to the rear and fitted with a lightweight stressed skin body shell of stark simplicity, this car was 150 lbs lighter than the regular Cape products and was capable of a top speed of around 110 mph with acceleration from zero to 60 mph in 11 seconds. In 1949 this was quite spectacular

performance and together with its safe handling characteristic made it a very successful competition car. Despite a short production run of 105 units ending in September 1950 it became the best known of all the Warwick built cars.

The success of the Silverstone in America showed the requirement in that market for a more powerful model and this led to the development of the Nash-Healey. This model was conceived out of a chance meeting in December 1949 between Donald Healey and George Mason, President of the Nash Kelvinator Corporation of America when both men were on board the Queen Elizabeth Ocean Liner en route to the United States. It was agreed that Nash engines, transmissions and rear axles would be supplied to Warwick for fitting to a slightly modified Healey chassis with a British body. The prototype car was completed in April 1950 and entered in the Italian classic Mille Migla road race. This test was successfully completed and was followed by entry in the French 24 hours endurance race at Le Mans where the car finished in fourth place overall and was the highest placed British car. Having proven the combination of British chassis and American mechanical units in competition, the decision to go into production with the model was taken in 1950 and the new car was launched at the London Motor Show in October that year with its American debut following at the Chicago Show in February 1951. Sold exclusively in the United States the Nash-Healey became the Warwick factory's largest volume production model with 508 units built between December 1950 and August 1954.

Because the Nash-Healey was for export only, it was decided to meet potential U.K. demand for a similar car by introducing a model known as the Sports convertible. This appeared at the 1951 London

Motor Show and was essentially a replica Nash-Healey with revised radiator grille and bumpers, and with a 3.0 litre six cylinder Alvis engine instead of the Nash unit. This was a very expensive high quality motor car and only 25 were built up to the end of production in late 1953.

With a full order book for the Nash-Healey, the Company was in good shape and Donald Healey and his team now began to give serious thought to the development of what they saw as a new concept in sports car design. Two important factors were to influence the new design. Firstly, the world sports car market was limited to either expensive models such as the Jaguar XK types or to fairly modestly priced designs of good saloon car performance typified by the MG range, and Donald Healey realised that here there was a sales gap waiting to be filled. Secondly, the expensive Riley mechanical units which had been the mainstay of Healey production were due to cease manufacture in the fairly near future and replacements would have to be found. With these considerations in mind the new car was planned as a less expensive, straightforward, high performance vehicle capable of being built in larger numbers than the Warwick factory had hitherto attempted.

The first problem requiring resolution was the supply of mechanical units. The Austin A90 Atlantic engine was of proven reliability following the seven days and nights record breaking endurance run at Indianapolis in April 1949 and was readily available together with gearbox, rear axle and front suspension assemblies from Austin A70/90 model ranges, and so the decision was quickly taken to use all these high volume production components. Having fixed the mechanical specification, the next step was to design a suitable chassis. Following the Healey design philosophy this was a simple but strong ladder type frame with square section parallel side members set 17 inches apart by cross members and braced by a cruciform centre member and welded in floor plates. Front and rear scuttle structures were also welded to the basic frame to enhance rigidity and torsional stiffness, the front unit being triangulated by struts running forward to the point where the substantial front suspension towers are carried on the side members. The whole structure was very strong without being overweight and provided the rigid frame which Donald Healey regarded as an essential element in achieving good and safe handling qualities in a high performance car. With only minor modifications to suit the installation of the later six cylinder engines and improved rear suspension, this frame remained fundamentally unchanged throughout the production life of the Big Healey in all its variations, ending in the BJ8 Mk III 3000.

The most striking feature of the new car was the body design which marked a radical change from traditional British sports car styling with its usual exposed running boards, exposed head lamps, cut-away doors and slab petrol tanks. The new car was clad in smooth panels with no extraneous fittings to mar an aerodynamically clean shell and was far superior in appearance to the slab sided contemporary Jaguar XK and Triumph models. It had a roomy cockpit, comfortable individual seats and a large lockable luggage compartment which also housed the spare wheel. Conceived by Donald Healey and translated into feasible actuality by stylist Gerry Coker, the design was quite outstanding and well ahead of its time, so much so, that it was capable of accepting the subtle changes introduced over the next 15 years made necessary by the specification

revisions to power unit and seating arrangements, without losing its fundamental character. After the passage of more than thirty years since its conception, the Big Healey in all its forms still looks marvellous and is today only slightly dated by its marginally narrower aspect than is current fashion. A sensational design which in the Author's opinion has not been bettered by a volume production sports car.

Initially presented as the Healey 100, the car was announced at the London Motor Show in October 1952 and became the sensation of the Show, despite the presence of many other very expensive and exotic creations. Interest in the car was such that the volume of orders received was quite beyond the capacity of the Warwick factory and this fact came to the attention of Leonard Lord, Chief Executive of the Austin Motor Company, the supplier of the major mechanical assemblies. Realising the sales potential of the car as an addition to his product range, Lord approached Donald Healey with the proposal that Austin take over the manufacture and distribution of the car, backing it up with their world wide Sales and Service network. An agreement was reached between the two men and the car was re-named and re-badged "Austin-Healey 100" overnight. A new marque was born!

The significant result of this agreement was that many more enthusiasts were able to buy a Healey designed car than would have been the case had production been limited to Warwick capability. The pleasure of owning and driving a thoroughbred sports car was opened up to a much larger market than would have been the case otherwise.

At a U.K. launch price of £850 exclusive of taxes the Austin-Healey 100 was still not a particularly cheap car, but it

substantially undercut the Jaguar XK 120 (£1130), the Alvis-Healey Convertible (£1400) and the Tickford and Abbott Healeys (£1200 bracket). The MG TD was £530, so that the original price objective was neatly achieved. To put these prices into perspective, it should be appreciated that in these post war years, a gross annual salary of around £1000 per year was regarded as exceptionally good.

Also at this time there was heavy emphasis on export sales and so whilst the car enjoyed an enthusiastic reception at home, the great majority of production was programmed for the United States after volume production began in May 1953. By July, the budget production of 100 cars per week was achieved and it became apparent that the purchasing power of the Austin Buying department could effect some significant economies in manufacturing costs. As a result, a reduction of £100 on the basic price of the car was announced which made it very competitive against the MG and TR models.

The first changes to the "100" came in the Summer of 1955 when several detail improvements were introduced, the most important of which was a much better gearbox which was to continue on the later six cylinder cars. Production continued at Longbridge until the annual summer holiday shut down at the end of July, 1956, when after a total of 14 612 cars, the last "100" was built.

Because the Austin-Healey was dependent upon volume produced BMC mechanical units it was inevitably effected by design and manufacturing considerations attaching to these components. The ageing four cylinder A90 engine was due to be phased out of production as part of a power unit rationalisation programme and a new six cylinder unit of similar displacement be introduced for installation in the large BMC saloon car ranges. The new "C" series engine first appeared in the Austin A90 Westminster Saloon in late 1954 and was tried experimentally in an Austin-Healey 100 in 1955. Installation required some minor front end chassis modifications and a repositioned radiator which dictated a revision to the bonnet line to give clearance over the radiator top tank and longer engine. Concurrent with these changes the rear body and seating arrangements were revised to provide a pair of jump seats which Donald Healey saw as an essential feature necessary to widen the market appeal of the car. These seating changes required that the rear axle be moved a couple of inches backwards and this was achieved by repositioning the spring hangers so that the chassis frame was not radically altered in this area. The extra body length resulting from this change was taken up by a corresponding increase in the length of the doors so that overall the side view of the car was not significantly changed, except for the appearance of external door handles. The folding windscreen of the 100 was abandoned in favour of a fixed screen and the bonnet lid was hinged at the rear instead of at the front as on the four cylinder cars. The new four seating arrangements meant that both the spare wheel and battery locations had to be revised and relocated into the boot which reduced the luggage capacity somewhat. The fuel filler was relocated to the top of the rear shroud behind the cockpit opening.

The new 100-6 was put into production at Longbridge in August 1956 following straight on from the discontinued 100 and was announced to the public in September 1956. The standard model now fitted with the improved A105 engine developed from the A90 unit was offered with pressed steel disc wheels instead of the regular wire wheels

of the 100, although these were available as a regular production option. Overdrive, heater and all the other standard features on the 100 also became option fit so that the price of the basic 100-6 at £762 was considerably cheaper than the superseded car, but to bring the car up to comparable specification increased the price to a significant margin over the 100.

Reaction to the new car was somewhat mixed since not only was overall performance slightly inferior to the previous model, but it was nearly 400 lb heavier which made it rather less nimble in its handling. It was also facing increased competition from the MG and TR model ranges. Fortunately an answer to the performance problem was in hand in the form of a redesigned cylinder head and induction system to give the engine a power lift from 102 bhp to 117 bhp. This improved engine was introduced concurrent with the shift of production from Longbridge to "The Sports Car Factory" at Abingdon in the late summer of 1957, and was announced in December of that year. This change of assembly location must have substantially increased manufacturing costs since the painted and partly trimmed bodies now had to be transported nearly 70 miles from Jensen at West Bromwich to Abingdon, rather than the twelve miles to Longbridge. Additionally, the power units had to be carried a similar distance from Morris Engines at Coventry and one wonders how these costs were absorbed into the only modest £55 price increment for such an improved car.

With a top speed increase of 8 mph and a whole second off the standing quarter mile time, the car was seen to be a much better performer and sales improved significantly. In order to meet a continuing demand from the major North American market for a car similar in concept to the original

"100", a two seat version of the 100-6 was introduced after the move to Abingdon and this model was announced in the summer of 1958. This derivative retained the smaller boot lid and rear shroud panels of the two plus two model revised to suit the reduced cockpit opening and in most respects it closely resembled the 100 in silhouette. There was also a reversion to twin six volt batteries and the spare wheel was relocated to give much improved boot capacity. At this time, both cars were equally priced at £817, less taxes. Production of both versions of the 100-6 models continued in parallel from March 1958, except for a four month period between May and August when building of the two plus two car was suspended for unknown reasons, until run out in May 1959. A combined Longbridge and Abingdon total of 14 436 100-6 models were built of which 4150 were the two seat version. Of the Abingdon built cars, 7859 were exported to the United States, which illustrates the importance of this market in justifying the manufacture of British sports cars.

As part of the continual BMC development programme, the "C" series engine power was lifted in early 1959 by increasing its displacement from 2639 cc to 2912 cc and raising the compression ratio from 8.5:1 to 9.0:1. This engine carrying the original "gallery inlet manifold" cylinder head was fitted to the Austin A110 and Wolseley Saloon cars, but exclusively for the Healey, the improved six port head from the Abingdon built 100-6 cars was specified. This bigger engine delivered 124 bhp and was introduced on the Austin-Healey from March 1959 build.

Fitted with the new three litre engine, production of the new car followed straight on from the 100-6 and was announced as the Austin-Healey 3000 on 1st July 1959. At first sight there was little visible difference over the superseded car, but performance was much enhanced with top speed up to 114 mph together with correspondingly improved acceleration. To cope with the improved performance 11$\frac{1}{4}$" Girling disc brakes replaced the front drum brakes of previous Big Healeys. Wire wheels, overdrive and heater remained as production options as did the hard-top from the 100-6. Price was increased to £829 for the basic two plus two car which was now £5 dearer than the still available two seat derivative. The retrospectively known 3000 Mk I continued in production until May 1961 with a total of 13 650 of both derivatives built of which 12 542 went to the United States.

In order to sustain demand in this important market several specification changes were introduced in this month. Visual changes were confined to a restyled radiator grille and bonnet lid aperture grille with vertical bars in contrast to the previous horizontal bars and the addition of a ''Mk II'' to the identification badges. The very significant change for this model was to the power unit which was given a further power lift to a claimed 132 bhp. This was achieved by the use of a higher lift camshaft with revised valve timing and the fitting of three SU HS4 carburettors instead of the two HD6 units. Both two plus two and two seat versions were offered at unchanged basic prices over the Mk I models. As before, overdrive, wire wheels and other features were offered as optional extras.

Unfortunately the 3000 Mk II was not particularly well received. Performance was not substantially enhanced and unskilled people ran into difficulties with the triple carburettor fuel system and so after ten months production and 5450 cars built, 5107 of which went to America, extensive and far reaching changes were made to the Big Healey. Realising the need to correct the shortcomings of the

car, within months of the launch, the Healey Company initiated a comprehensive design study into ways of improving its comfort and general customer appeal. The two seat car was phased out, the engine reverted to a twin carburettor fuel system from the 3000 Mk I, but with a revised camshaft retained virtually the same power output. The new gearbox with top mounted gear lever introduced on the Mk II as a running change in November 1961 was carried over and a completely new and improved folding hood complimented by wind-up windows was also featured. Great care was taken over the design of the new hood which could now be easily erected and folded single handed. It was also quite weatherproof and overcame previous criticisms of earlier models. The body changes consequent upon the new hood, wind-up side windows, wrap around windscreen and opening quarter lights meant that some pre-production built cars had to be sent down the Abingdon production lines whilst 3000 Mk II production was still running. These cars were built in early 1962 before production of the new model was phased in from March 1962. It could be said that in order to preserve correct Mark numbering sequence, this car should have been badged a Mk III, but in order to avoid lengthy homologation checks, which could have delayed its introduction, it was designated as a Mk II

Austin Healey

Convertible, later becoming widely known amongst enthusiasts as the Mk 11A.

At its launch in August 1962, the price of the basic car was £865, an increase of £36 over the Mk I and Mk II models. Overdrive, wire wheels and heater remained as option fit with the further option of a brake servo. Maximum speed was lifted to 117 mph. The 3000 Convertible was in production until November 1963 with a total of 6113 built, 5019 going to United States markets.

When planning the Convertible model, a comprehensive package of improvements had been planned, but introduction as a whole would have delayed manufacture for an unacceptable period and so some elements were held over for the next phase. These features were introduced in two stages on the final 3000 derivative known as the Mk III, which was announced in the U.K. in February 1964, although production had begun in the previous November.

The 3000 Mk III was the most powerful and refined of all regular production Austin-Healey cars. Externally there were initially no changes from the previous model, except for the Mk III additions to the badges. The engine was given a further power lift to 148 bhp by means of yet another revision to cam profiles and timing and the fitting of two 30 degree semi-downdraught SU HD8 carburettors. An improved four box silencing and exhaust system which also improved ground clearance was fitted. This system did not materially reduce engine power, but was capable of ensuring that the car met forthcoming noise regulations. Inside, there was an all new full width wood facia and a transmission tunnel console. There was also a change to the rear seats by the provision of a fold down back panel to give a flat load carrying platform. This most powerful series production Healey was also much the fastest, being capable of 120 mph and a standing quarter mile in 15.6 seconds, both values slightly better than the 100S which was built as an out and out competition car. All these improvements naturally involved a cost element and the price of the basic car was increased by £50 to £915. Overdrive, wire wheels and heater remained as regular production options at extra cost, but the brake servo became a standard fit.

In May 1964 what was probably the most important item in the planned product improvement package was introduced. The rear frame was modified to permit more rear axle vertical travel for improved ground clearance and softer rear springs were fitted. To resist wind-up of these softer springs, forward facing radius arms were fitted to the rear axle. The Panhard rod previously specified for all Big Healeys was deleted at this change point.

The last highly visual change to the Big Healey came in April 1965 when separate side marker and turn indicator lamps were introduced to the front and rear, with panel pressing changes being made to accept the larger lamp lenses. The rear reflectors were relocated to small brackets on the rear bumper blade.

By now it was becoming clear that proposed American occupant protection standards and emission control legislation were posing a severe threat to the continued production of the Big Healey, especially as no agreement could be reached with BMC as to either possible product action to meet these requirements or for a suitable replacement model. Consequently, production of the Mk III 3000 was gradually run down and manufacture finally ended at Abingdon in December 1967, although two left-hand drive cars were built in January 1968 (which date excluded them

from the American market) and the very last car, Chassis number 43 036, to U.K. specification was built in March 1968. The last U.S. specification car was shipped to Jacksonville.

A total of 17 704 regular production BJ8 cars were built of which 15 407 went to North American markets.

During the 11 year production life of the big six cylinder Austin-Healeys, an extensive Racing and Rally programme was followed for both product development and promotional purposes. Quite early on it was agreed that the race cars would be the responsibility of the Warwick factory whilst the Rally events would be handled by the BMC Competitions Department at Abingdon. Many of the developments made for the race cars were carried over to the rally machines to make them very formidable contenders in International events. Results gradually improved until in 1960 Pat Moss and Ann Wisdom won the Liege-Rome-Liege with car URX 727, the first time any British Works team had achieved outright victory in this most demanding of all rally competitions. Thereafter the run of successes continued with wins in successive years in the Alpine and Tulip Rallys and overall first place in the 1964 Spa-Sofia-Liege event. Throughout this period many class wins and overall placings were achieved to establish the Big Healey as a superb sporting machine capable to taking on the worlds best and expensive competition cars.

But despite these successes there was one international event which BMC were unable to win with the Big Healey and this was the U.K. RAC Rally! Despite not being really suited to the British event, the cars finished second in 1961, 1962, 1964 and 1965, victory in the last event being snatched from Timo Makinen in the closing stages by Rauno

Aaltanon driving one of the works Mini Cooper S cars. Regulation changes for 1966 meant that no works 3000 cars were entered although two private entries took part, but without significant success. For the 1967 event a special Group 6 class for prototype cars was introduced and this gave BMC the opportunity to prepare and enter what was to be the ultimate 3000 Rally Car with an all aluminium engine developing around 200 bhp at its Minilite road wheels. This car was rebuilt from a 1964 BJ8 Rally car previously registered ARX 92B which had been purchased from the works by Peter Browning who had succeeded Stuart Turner as Competitions Manager. Re-registered PWB 67 the car never saw competition as the event had to be cancelled by order of the Ministry of Agriculture following an outbreak of Foot and Mouth disease. Thus ended the Rally career of the 3000.

During the production life of the Big Healey the Healey family were continually examining ideas to extend the market appeal of the model and with the support of the BMC management a design study was initiated in late 1963 into the feasibility of producing a fixed head derivative of the 3000 along the lines of MG and Jaguar models. Two designs were produced. One, based on a normal BJ8 chassis by the Austin stylist, the late Dick Burzi was rather simpler in concept than the other proposal by Donald and Geoffrey Healey based on a Sebring race car chassis with competition engine and running gear. It was thought that this version to be called the 3000S would be built with a high quality interior in limited numbers as a very high performance model whilst the Burzi design would be offered as a 3000 Coupe to appeal to a higher volume market. An unfortunate interpretation of the cost estimates involved in producing these models taken together with already high investment made by BMC for the MGB GT and MGC tooling meant that the proposal died. Fortunately the two examples survive and are in fine condition in the good and careful hands of Don Humphires.

The final exercise in the search to find a model to continue the Big Healey model line was a widened version of the 3000 body shell powered by the Rolls Royce 4 litre R engine from the Austin Westminster Van den Plas model. Only three examples were built when BMC cancelled the project in April 1967, probably due to the difficulties anticipated in meeting forthcoming American exhaust emission and occupant protection standards coupled with a re-appraisal of the model range

following the formation of British Motor Holdings arising from the merger of BMC with Jaguar. The three cars were sold but again happily survive in good hands. And so the Big Healey ended in December 1967 and the Healey family turned their attention to their new project which was to become the Jensen Healey which eventually appeared in 1972.

But it was not quite the end of the Austin-Healey. The Sprite continued as a Healey up to December 31st 1970 when it

became the Austin Sprite until production ended in the summer of 1971. All vehicles produced bearing the Healey name had to be sold retail by 30th June 1971 in order to comply with the licencing agreement with the family.

EVOLUTION

Evolution

The big six cylinder Austin-Healey cars are directly derived from the original four cylinder Longbridge built 100 model and for the first twelve months of the eleven year production run the 100-6 was built down the same assembly lines, until manufacture was transferred in August 1957 to the Abingdon Sports Car Factory. By the time production of the Big Healey ended in December 1967 there had been four revisions to engine specification and body style was confined to a 2 + 2 Convertible configuration.

Type codes followed on from the BN1 and BN2 series of the 100, beginning with BN4 through BN6 and BN7 to BT7, BJ7 and finally BJ8. These codes are derived from the BMC Standards for defining passenger car identifications. The letter "B" indicates an engine displacement in the range 2000 to 2999 cc whilst the "N", "T" or "J" characterises the body styles as either "Two Seat Tourer", "Four Seat Tourer", or "Convertible" and the digits 4, 6, 7, 8 refer to the model series. Left-hand drive versions carry the letter "L" after the "BN" code, thus BJ8L. It

appears that BMC planners of the day did not read their Standards Manual because the car known as BN4 should in truth be BT4 whilst the BN6 was correctly identified. The gaps in number sequence are filled by two cars, the BN3, only one example of which was built in 1955 as a prototype of the BN4 and which fortunately survives in Australia, and by the BN5, again a one-off car built in 1957, the fate of which remains unknown.

When the BN4 was introduced in September 1956 many of the features which had been standard specification on the 100 became regular production options in order to hold down the base price of the car and maximise the profitability of these features and this policy continued through to the end of production of the BJ8 Mk 111 3000 model. The various models embraced by the generic term "Big Healey" were introduced in response to the continual need to improve both performance and comfort as demanded by changing market requirements and occasionally because of the need to comply with legislative requirements.

The most significant model and specification changes were introduced at the following points.

August 1956.
Manufacture of BN4 100-6 2 + 2 car with 2639 cc 102 bhp engine begins at Longbridge in the Chassis number range 22598 to 50758.

August 1957.
Manufacture of BN4 transferred to Abingdon with production start up in November.

November 1957.
Abingdon build of 2 + 2 BN4 commences at Chassis 50759 with improved 2639 cc 117 bhp engine and runs to Chassis 62190 within Allocation Numbers 501 to 2441.

March 1958.
BN6 2 seater production begins at Chassis Number 501 running to 4650 at last car. General Specification as BN4.

April 1958.
BN4 production ceases at Chassis 62190.

September 1958.
BN4 2 + 2 model resumes production at Chassis 68527 and runs to Chassis 77766 within Allocation Numbers 2442 to 4744.

March 1959.
Production switches from 100-6 BN4 and BN6 models to the BN7 and BT7 3000 model series. Visually similar to the superseded 100-6 models, but fitted with an increased displacement engine of 2912 cc developing 124 bhp and 11 1/4" diameter Girling disc brakes for the front wheels.

Build of the first car, a red home market model carrying Chassis Number BT101 was begun on 2nd March, but was not completed until 22nd April by which time many other cars had been built and passed off, including the first BN two seat car. This was BN186, a blue USA spec car completed on 13th March.

May 1961.
Last 3000 Mk 1 car built. This was a British Racing Green home market car with Chassis Number 13750 completed on 15th May 1961.

In the same month production of the 3000 Mk II series had begun at Chassis Number 13751 carrying straight on in sequence from the Mk 1. This first car was a blue USA spec model also completed on the 15th May.

November 1961.
New and improved gearbox with top mounted centre change together with new glass fibre transmission cover introduced as a running change on BT7 models at Chassis Number 15881, a North American car built 20th November.

January 1962.
The new gearbox introduced as a running change on two seat models at Chassis Number BN7 16039, again a car for North America. In the same month the first four pre-production BJ convertibles were built down the Abingdon assembly line. These

cars numbered BJ7 17551-4 were completed on the 30th of the month and were all to Canadian market specification.

March 1962.
Last BN7, Chassis Number 18888 built. This car was a white USA car, completed on 23rd March.

June 1962.
Last BT7, Chassis Number 19853 built. This was a red home market car, completed 8th June.

Immediately following this car, the first regular production BJ7 Convertible was built. A blue Canadian market model, Chassis Number 19854, this car was completed on the 15th June, 1962.

June 1963.
At car BJ7 24637, stronger 60 spoke wire wheels instead of the original 48 spoke type were introduced as a running change. This was an American market car finished in blue on 28th June.

November 1963.
The last BJ7 car was built. Finished British Racing Green with Chassis Number 25314, this car was completed on the 19th November for the home market.

Production of the new BJ8 3000 Mk III Phase 1 model then began, following on in Chassis Number sequence from the last BJ7, but in fact this "first car" was not completed until June 1964. This was a red, home market car. For unknown production reasons, car numbers 25316 and 25317 were completed in December and October and thereafter volume began to build up slowly but steadily.

May 1964.
Phase 2 models of the BJ8 production began after 1390 cars had been built with the introduction at Chassis 26705 of the revised rear suspension package. At the same time, stronger splined hubs with 8 TPI threads for the knock-on caps were introduced. This car finished in blue was completed on 20th May and was to American spec. for a personal export customer.

April 1965.
Phase 3 models having improved separate turn and side marker lamps were introduced at Chassis Number 31336. Both this car and 31337 were sent to the Competitions Department so that the first Phase 3 BJ8 to be sold to the public was 31338, a blue American market car, completed on 5th April.

January 1967.
A new and unusual colour was introduced. Metallic golden beige was the only other metallic paint finish offered on the Austin-Healey and was used on 553 cars, of which 510 went to the USA. First car in this colour was chassis 40190 built for the UK market on 20th January and the last was 43025, built 22nd November for the Donald Healey Motor Company. The two trim colours available with golden beige were red or black.

July 1967.
One car, Chassis 42230 was built to special order with silver grey paint and a red interior with seats piped in white.

December 1967.
Assembly of the last car for the United States was completed on December 21st. This was chassis 43004 finished in BRG, despatched to Jacksonville on 16th January 1968. All other cars up to Chassis 43025 with the exceptions of 43000 and 43007

had already been completed by this time. Owing to shortage of parts these two cars stood in the assembly shop until completed on the 11th and 1st January respectively. Although to US Specification, these could not be sold in America since new emission regulations came into effect on 1st January and to qualify for sale, cars had to be certified finish built before this date.

The very last BJ8 was chassis 43026, finished in white and built in the "Show Shop". It was completed on 14th March 1968.

Special Market Requirement
For the French market, special 2850 cc engines were built. These are identified by engine numbers prefixed 29FF for the BJ7 and 29KF for the BJ8.

SPECIFICATION

Specifications

Type codes

Austin-Healey 100-6.

Type BN4: Open 2 + 2 seats
Type BN6: 2 Seat version

Austin-Healey 3000

Type BN7: Open 2 seater
Type BT7: Open 2 + 2 seats

Austin-Healey 3000 Mk II

Type BN7: Open 2 seater
Type BT7: Open 2 + 2 seats

Austin-Healey 3000 Mk II Convertible Type BJ7: 2 + 2 Seat Convertible
Austin-Healey 3000 Mk III
Convertible

Type BJ8: 2 + 2 Seat Convertible

Built

100-6 BN4 with 102 bhp engine built at Longbridge in the period August 1956 to August 1957.
100-6 BN4 with 117 bhp engine, BN6 and all 3000 models built at the MG Plant at Abingdon between November 1957 and December 1967.

Production Volumes

6045 Longbridge built BN4 cars
All other production at Abingdon.
4241 BN4
4150 BN6
13650 3000 Mk I
5450 3000 Mk II
6113 3000 Mk II Convertible (3000 Mk 11A)
1390 3000 Mk III Phase I
4631 3000 Mk III Phase 2
11691 3000 Mk III Phase 3

Configuration

Front engine, manual transmission with optional overdrive, rear wheel drive, open sports type body.

Specifications 100-6 BN4 (First Series)

Engine	Morris "C" Series 6 cylinder push-rod ohv unit with watercooled cast iron block and head. Produced for use in Austin A90 Westminster and Wolseley Saloons.
Bore	79.4mm (3.125ins); Stroke 89mm (3.5ins):
Displacement	2639cc (161.1 cu ins)
Compression ratio	8.25:1
Max Power	102 bhp at 4600 rpm
Max Torque	142 lb ft at 2400 rpm
Fuel system	Two horizontal SU H4 Carburettors with pancake type air filters, carried on cast-in "gallery type" inlet manifold. SU electric high pressure pump feed from 54.6 litre (12 gallons) fuel tank.
Lubricating oil capacity	6.8 litres (12 pints)
Cooling system capacity	11.37 litres (20 pints)
Clutch	Single dry plate, 23cm (9ins) diameter.
Gearbox	Four speed and reverse with optional fit Laycock Overdrive unit, operative on third and fourth gears.
Oil capacity	2.27 litres (4 pints) without overdrive, 2.98 litres (5¼ pints) with overdrive.
Gearbox ratios	1st 3.07; 2nd 1.91; 3rd, 1.33; 4th, 1.00; Reverse 4.17.
Overdrive ratio	0.778
Rear Axle	Hypoid bevel three quarter floating type with 4.10:1 ratio (10/41 tooth combination) for overdrive fitted cars. For non-overdrive cars 3.91 ratio (11/43 tooth combination).
Oil capacity	1.7 litres (3 pints).
Overall Gear Ratio:	Without Overdrive: 12.02; 7.48; 5.21; 3.91 with 12.02 reverse. With Overdrive: 12.61; 7.84; 5.47 (4.25 with O/D); 4.10 (3.19 with O/D) and 17.05 reverse.
Road speeds at 1000 rpm	
Engine speed	Without overdrive, top gear: 18.9 mph With overdrive, top gear: 23.2 mph
Steering	Cam and Peg steering gear with three piece track rod. Steering ratio, 14:1 Steering Wheel diameter, 16.5 ins.
Suspension	
Front	Independent by double wishbone arms and coil springs controlled by double action lever arm dampers functioning as the top link. Anti-roll bar cross connection.
Rear	Semi elliptic leaf springs controlled by double action lever arm dampers. Panhard rod for lateral control.
Brakes	Girling hydraulic 11 inch diameter drum brake system with 2¼ inch wide shoes.
Wheels and tyres	Pressed steel ventilated disc wheels as standard specification with 48 wire spoke centre lock wheels as option fit. 5.90x15 tyres on 15x4½ J rims.

Chassis	Steel Box section longitudinal side members with cruciform centre section cross bracing and front and rear cross members. Integral welded body framing.
Electrical System	12 volt positive earth system. Single 50 ampere hour battery. Twin windscreen wipers. Twin horns.
Bodywork	Occasional four seater two door open sports tourer with all weather protection. Flush panelled steel and aluminium coachwork with wide opening doors fitted with outside handles. Fixed position laminated glass windscreen. Full length tonneau cover. Connolly leather facings to seats. Duo tone paint finish available on request.

Main dimensions and weight

Overall length	4.00m (13ft 1$\frac{1}{2}$ins)
Overall width	1.54m (5ft 0$\frac{1}{2}$ins)
Height over scuttle	0.94m (2ft 11$\frac{3}{4}$ins)
Height over hood	1.24m (4ft 2ins)
Wheelbase	2.34m (7ft 8ins)
Front track	1.24m (4ft 1ins)
Rear track	1.27m (4ft 2ins)
Ground clearance	0.14m (5$\frac{1}{2}$ins)
Kerb weight	1099 kg (2422lbs)

Specification 100-6 BN4 (Second Series)

Specifications generally as first series except:

Engine	Revised cylinder head with separate induction ports and cast aluminium bolt-on induction manifold.
Compression ratio	8.5:1
Fuel system	Two semi downdraught SU HD6 carburettors.
Max. power	117 bhp at 4750 rpm
Max. torque 149 lb ft at 3000 rpm	
Optional extras	Radio, hardtop, heater, overdrive, (With wire wheels and with overdrive, Road Speed Tyres were a mandatory option) These options were also available on the first series cars.

Specification 100-6 BN6

Specification generally as for second series BN4 but with two seat bodywork. Two 6 volt batteries of 57 ampere hour capacity located behind heel board as on BN1 and BN2 models.

Kerb weight with wire wheels and overdrive	1105 kg (2436 lb)

Specifications 3000 Mk I BN7 and BT7

Specifications generally as BN4 and BN6 except:

Engine

Displacement	2912cc
Bore	83.36 mm (3.28 ins)
Stroke	88.9 mm (3.5 ins)
Compression ratio	9.0:1
Max. power	124 bhp at 4600 rpm
Max. torque	175 lb ft at 3000 rpm

Clutch — Single dry plate, 25.4 cm (10 ins) diameter

Gearbox — Revised ratios four speed and reverse gearbox with optional fit Laycock Overdrive unit operative on third and fourth gears.

Gearbox rations	1st 2.93; 2nd 2.05; 3rd 1.31; 4th 1.00
Reverse	3.78
Overdrive ratio	0.822

Rear axle — Revised ratio for both overdrive and non-overdrive fitted cars.

Without overdrive ratio	3.545:1 (11/39)
With overdrive, ratio	3.91 (11/43)

Overall Gear Ratios:

Without overdrive	10.39; 7.28; 4.64; 3.545 and 13.40; 1 reverse
With overdrive	11.45; 8.03; 5.12 (4.20 with O/d); 3.91 (3.21 with O/d and 14.78 reverse)

Road Speeds at 1000 rpm engine speed:

Without overdrive, top gear	20.9 mph
With overdrive, top gear	23.1 mph

Brakes — Girling disc front brakes, 11$^{1/4}$ ins diameter. 11 ins diameter x 2$^{1/4}$ inch wide rear drum brakes.

Kerb Weights — 2 Seater with disc wheels and without overdrive, 1030 kg (2381 lbs)
2 seater with wire wheels and overdrive, 1092 kg (2408 lbs)
2 + 2 Seater with disc wheels and without overdrive, 1077 kg (2375 lbs)
2 + 2 Seater with wire wheels and overdrive, 1085 kg (2393 lbs)

Specification 3000 Mk II, BN7 and BT7

Specifications generally as for Mk I except:

Engine — Revised camshaft and three SU HS4 carburettors to raise output to 132 bhp at 4750 rpm with 167 lb ft torque at 3000 rpm

Gearbox	Running change at BT7 15881 and BN7 16039 introduced improved gearbox with top mounted selectors and central gearlever. Concurrently a new glass fibre transmission tunnel cover giving improved cockpit insulation was also introduced.
Bodywork	Revised pattern front radiator grille and bonnet top aperture grille with vertical bars instead of the previous horizontal bars. Bonnet badge revised to incorporate "Mk II".

Specification 3000 Mk II Convertible, BJ7

Specification generally as Mk II BT7 except:

Engine	Reversion to twin carburettor induction system with 2 SU HS6 instruments and a further camshaft revision to maintain power at virtually the BN7/BT7 level at 131 bhp at 4750 rpm with 165 lb ft torque at 3000 rpm.
Brakes	Optional servo assistance.
Wheels and tyres	The optional fit 48 spoke wire wheels replaced by 60 spoke type with 5J rims as a running change at Chassis number 24637.
Bodywork	New wrap-around windscreen with hinged opening quarter lights and wind-up glass windows to the doors. New fold-away hood with removeable backlight.
Kerb weight	Base car with disc wheels and without overdrive, 1080kg (2380 lbs).

Specification 3000 Mk III Convertible, BJ8, Phase 1

Specification generally as Mk II BJ7 except:

Engine	Similar to Mk II engine but with further revision to camshaft and 2 SU HD8 carburettors. Improved four silencer box exhaust system to give more ground clearance and to satisfy noise regulations. Output lifted to 148 bhp at 5250 rpm with 165 lb ft torque at 3500 rpm.
Clutch	$9^1/2$ in diameter (24 cm) diaphragm spring type.
Gearbox	As later BJ7 cars but with slightly revised ratios. 1st 2.64; 2nd 2.07; 3rd 1.31; 4th 1.00 with reverse 3.39.
Rear axle	Unchanged, but revisions to gearbox ratios affect overall ratios. These become:
Without Overdrive	9.35; 7.34; 4.63; 3.545 with 12.02 reverse.
With overdrive	10.3; 8.10; 5.11; (4.19 with O/D); 3.91 (3.21 with O/D) with 13.26 reverse.

Road Speeds at 1000 rpm engine speed:

Without overdrive, top gear: 20.8 mph

With overdrive, top gear   23.0 mph

Brakes   Servo assistance as standard fit.

Coachwork   Ambla trim to seat facings as standard with leather as option.
New full width wooden facia panel and long centre console between front seats.

Specification BJ8 Phase 2

Chassis   Rear end side members reduced in depth and strengthened to allow more rear axle vertical travel, softer rear springs, with revised profile to increase ground clearance and forward facing radius arms to resist spring wind-up introduced as running change at Chassis 26705.

Hubs   For wire wheel fitted cars, improved splined hubs fitted with 8 T.P.I. nut threads instead of the previous 12 T.P.I. threads. This change concurrent with rear suspension and axle change.

Specification BJ8 Phase 3

Specification as Phase 2 except:

Bodywork   Revisions to front and rear shroud panels to incorporate enlarged lenses at rear and separate side marker and side turn indicator lamps at the front.
This change introduced as a running change at Chassis 31336.

The Autocar
ROAD
TESTS

No. 1612

AUSTIN-
HEALEY
100 SIX

A good-looking car from all angles. When dismantled the hood and supports fold completely away behind the back seat rest

SEVERAL quantity-production sports cars are made today by the larger firms, and they incorporate power and transmission units similar to those used in their more sedate products. They have performance equal to that of pre-war specialist cars, but their price remains reasonable. The new Austin-Healey 100 Six, a logical development of its popular predecessor, falls into this category. The 2.6-litre four-cylinder engine has been replaced by the C series, 102 b.h.p., six-cylinder unit of fractionally smaller capacity, as fitted in the Austin A.105 saloon, and there are two additional forward-facing occasional seats for children.

Externally there is little noticeable difference between the old and the new—a sure indication of good basic design. The air inlet on the bonnet top and re-styled radiator grille —rather more ornate than in the past—bearing the unmistakable imprint of Longbridge, distinguish the 100 Six from the former Hundred at a quick glance. The wheelbase has been extended by 2in to 7ft 8in, and this extra length sensibly has been incorporated in the door opening, thereby making for easier entry and exit. A fixed windscreen, neatly shaped and of quite large area, is now fitted.

The Austin engine is exceptionally smooth, and its useful torque range extends to very low crankshaft speeds. Thus the revised Austin-Healey is even more tractable than its predecessor, and is as much at home pottering about on a shopping expedition as speeding along *routes nationales* and *autobahnen*. For purely experimental purposes, one can move off from a standstill in top gear and accelerate in this ratio to over 100 m.p.h. without protest from engine or transmission.

The Laycock-de Normanville overdrive, which was fitted to the car tested, is an optional extra and operates on third and top gears only. It is allied with a 4.1 to 1 rear axle ratio, which confers an overdrive ratio of 3.19 to 1, whereas in standard form the final drive is 3.91 to 1.

Whilst many buyers will prefer to pay extra for the overdrive, the standard ratios would probably allow maximum speed to be reached more quickly and thus more often. During the road test it became standard practice to use first gear from rest, and to change up to second immediately the car was moving; normal third was engaged at approximately 40 m.p.h., and it was then simply a matter of flicking the facia-mounted overdrive switch to obtain overdrive third, a ratio which embodies a useable speed range between 15 and 90 m.p.h.

After accelerating in this ratio, little was gained by reverting to normal top (with simultaneous movements of gear lever and overdrive switch), and it soon became customary to shift from overdrive third to overdrive top. Downward changes depended upon circumstances—either lever engagement of overdrive third, or an electric selection of normal top. There was almost imperceptible lag during the engagement of overdrive. Upward changes are made—and

The six-cylinder Healey is recognizable by the new-styled radiator grille and the air inlet vent on the bonnet top. The flashing signals are incorporated in the side lights

indeed are much smoother—if the throttle is kept open, as recommended by the makers. Half the pleasure of driving a high-geared car is lost if the gear box ratios and control are unsatisfactory. With 23.18 m.p.h. per 1,000 r.p.m. in overdrive top, the Austin-Healey is quite high-geared, but its gear box scores full marks on both counts and one welcomes excuses to use it.

With hood and side screens erect, the 100 Six proved to have about the same mean and one-direction maxima as its predecessor, when tested by *The Autocar* in September of 1953, but the car under review had covered only a nominal mileage, and might well improve on this when more fully run-in. It is understood that the same car, subsequent to

Super Profile

AUSTIN-HEALEY—
100 Six . . .

The doors, now wider, open almost at right angles; entry into the driving seat is easy; and reasonably so even when the all-weather equipment is in position. There are wide, deep map pockets in each door

The bonnet top is hinged at the rear and its lock is supplemented by two safety catches. Pancake air cleaners are fitted to the S.U. carburettors. On the right of the engine the distributor is easy to reach, and the sump breather pipe is led via the rocker cover to the rearmost air cleaner

our test, lapped the M.I.R.A. circuit in 2 min 15 sec (107 m.p.h.); and it is worth recalling that the four-cylinder car, which was the subject of our 1953 test, achieved a mean speed of 111 m.p.h. and a best speed in one direction of 119 m.p.h., after the windscreen had been removed and an aero screen and tonneau cover substituted. The 100 Six would doubtless react equally well to the same treatment. Although it has, on paper, some 12 b.h.p. in hand over the four-cylinder car, it weighs over three hundredweight more, and the acceleration figures are not quite so good. This may also result from differences in the torque curves of the two engines, and in the gear box ratios, the earlier car having a three-speed box with overdrive. Thus, although 80 m.p.h. from a standstill in 22.6 sec is creditable enough, the earlier car was more than 4½ sec quicker.

The combination of an unladen weight of 22 cwt., high gearing and a reasonable power-to-weight ratio provides the essentials for fast motoring with a moderate fuel consumption. In addition, it is difficult to drive this car to the stage where the crew become physically tired; it has, in fact, the traditional Seven League Boots. The suspension and road-holding are a combination of old and new, as is now expected with a modern sports car. There is little or no heeling over or tyre squeal on fast corners, and the ride is unexpectedly smooth, especially so on Continental *pavé*.

One is conscious of slight firmness only when travelling over indifferent surfaces with the tyres at the high pressures recommended for sustained fast cruising speeds. Steering characteristics are neutral as near as no matter, and one is able, on sharp bends, to promote a degree of oversteer at will by intelligent use of the throttle pedal. There is a satisfactory amount of self-centring action.

The clutch action is faultless; full throttle starts produced no slip, and at all times the engagement was smooth. The

Spare wheel and battery occupy much of the luggage boot. The locker lid is prevented from damaging the hood by a retaining wire cable. Separate reflectors are housed in streamlined fairings above the rear lamps. A light behind the bumper illuminates the rear number plate

pendant pedal is set at a comfortable angle, and only average pressure is called for. The three pedals seem unnecessarily close together, and it was not possible to indulge in "heel and toe" gear changes. Brake pedal pressure is light, except for full energy stops, and the brakes are adequate to the usable maximum speed. They are not prone to fade or grab. The parking brake lever is close to the driving seat, but causes no interference with the driver's movements, and is very efficient.

The general comfort of the car is praiseworthy, except that the leather-trimmed seat cushions are rather too short to support the thighs adequately, and shallow, so that the driver becomes rather conscious of the seat frame beneath after travelling some 200 miles. Backrests, which hinge forward to give access to the rear seats, are a little flimsy, and do not provide the stiff lateral support which one expects in this type of car. The angle of the backrests, however, is excellent, and they are tapered to allow plenty of elbow room.

As compared with the previous model, there is more foot room for the driver, and it is no longer necessary for him to rest the left foot on the clutch pedal. The layout suits a tall driver better than a short one, for the relationship between seat and pedals is such that a short person, having adjusted the seat so that he can reach the pedals comfortably, will find himself too close to the steering wheel.

The short, rigid gear lever, which protrudes from the left side of the gear box cover, is easy to reach and delightful to use. The movements between gears are short and precise, and the box is mechanically very quiet. The crew sit well down in the car, and there is excellent weather protection. The windscreen is a fixture, whereas the previous screen could be lowered along the scuttle to decrease frontal area during high-speed runs; and there are improved, rigid-framed sidescreens with sliding Perspex panels.

Raising and lowering the hood is a rather long and involved procedure. It would be impossible to raise the hood in the event of a sudden shower without the crew getting wet, and this would be more than ever true if the driver were travelling alone and had to do the job himself. Once up, however, it is extremely taut, and the leading edge of the hood is particularly safely secured to the top of the windscreen frame. With hood and sidescreens erect, the car is commendably quiet up to 80 m.p.h.; above this, wind noise becomes much more evident and conversation correspondingly more difficult.

AUSTIN-HEALEY 100 SIX

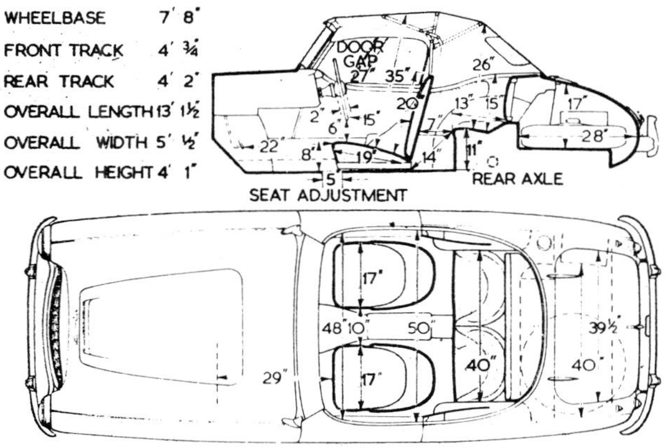
WHEELBASE 7' 8"
FRONT TRACK 4' ¾"
REAR TRACK 4' 2"
OVERALL LENGTH 13' 1½"
OVERALL WIDTH 5' ½"
OVERALL HEIGHT 4' 1"
DOOR GAP
SEAT ADJUSTMENT
REAR AXLE

Measurements in these ¼in to 1ft scale body diagrams are taken with the driving seat in the central position of fore and aft adjustment and with the seat cushions uncompressed

PERFORMANCE

ACCELERATION: from constant speeds.
Speed Range, Gear Ratios and Time in sec.

M.P.H.	*3.19 to 1	4.1 to 1	*4.25 to 1	5.46 to 1	7.84 to 1	12.61 to 1
10—30	—	7.7	—	5.8	4.2	3.4
20—40	10.2	7.7	7.6	5.8	4.0	—
30—50	10.6	8.0	7.8	5.8	4.9	—
40—60	11.8	8.3	8.1	6.5	—	—
50—70	12.6	8.8	8.7	7.9	—	—
60—80	14.7	10.6	10.7	—	—	—
70—90	19.2	15.3	16.0	—	—	—

*Overdrive.

From rest through gears to:

M.P.H.	sec.
30	4.3
50	9.3
60	12.9
70	17.5
80	22.6
90	32.3

Standing quarter mile, 18.8 sec.

SPEEDS ON GEARS:

Gear		M.P.H. (normal and max.)	K.P.H. (normal and max.)
O.D. Top	**(mean)**	**103**	**165**
	(best)	**107***	**172**
Top	**(mean)**	**98.5**	**158**
	(best)	**101**	**162**
O.D. 3rd		**80—95**	**129—153**
3rd		**60—73**	**97—117**
2nd		**40—50**	**64—80**
1st		**24—31**	**39—50**

*See text, page 684

TRACTIVE RESISTANCE: 16 lb per ton at 10 M.P.H.

TRACTIVE EFFORT:

	Pull (lb per ton)	Equivalent Gradient
Top	244	1 in 9.1
O.D. Third	402	1 in 5.5
Third	464	1 in 4.7
Second	579	1 in 3.7

BRAKES (at 30 m.p.h.):

Efficiency	Pedal Pressure (lb)
49 per cent	30
66 per cent	50
79 per cent	75
85 per cent	130

FUEL CONSUMPTION:
23.3 m.p.g. overall for 941 miles (12.12 litres per 100 km).
Approximate normal range: 20-27 m.p.g. (14-10 litres per 100 km).
Fuel, first grade.

WEATHER: Cloudy, slight headwind, dry tarmac surface.
Air temperature 58 deg F.
Acceleration figures are the means of several runs in opposite directions.
Tractive effort and resistance obtained by Tapley meter.
Model described in *The Autocar* of September 28, 1956.

SPEEDOMETER CORRECTION: M.P.H.

Car speedometer:	10	20	30	40	50	60	70	80	90	100
True speed:	13	20	29	38	48	58	68	78	87	96

DATA

PRICE (basic), with occasional four-seater body, **£762.**
British purchase tax, **£382 7s.**
Total (in Great Britain), **£1,144 7s.**
Extras: Heater **£23 5s** inc. P.T.
Overdrive: **£69 15s** inc. P.T.
Wire wheels and Road Speed tyres **£46 10s** inc. P.T.

ENGINE: Capacity: 2,639 c.c. (161 cu in).
Number of cylinders: 6.
Bore and stroke: 79.4 × 89.0 mm (3.125 × 3.5in).
Valve gear: overhead valves and pushrods.
Compression ratio: 8.25 to 1.
B.H.P.: 102 at 4,600 r.p.m. (B.H.P. per ton laden 81.1).
Torque: 142 lb ft at 2,400 r.p.m.
M.P.H. per 1,000 r.p.m. on top gear 18.08.
M.P.H. per 1,000 r.p.m. on overdrive 23.18.

WEIGHT: (with 5 gals fuel): 22 cwt (2,478 lb).
Weight disbribution (per cent): F, 49; R, 51.
Laden as tested: 25¾ cwt (2,803 lb).
Lb per c.c. (laden): 1.06.

BRAKES: Type: F, two-leading shoe; R, leading and trailing.
Method of operation: F, hydraulic; R, hydraulic.
Drum dimensions: F, 11in diameter; 2¼in wide. R, 11in diameter; 2¼in wide.
Lining area: F, 95 sq in. R, 95 sq in (151.8 sq in per ton laden).

TYRES: 5.90—15in.
Pressures (lb per sq in): F, 20; R, 23 (normal). F, 26; R, 29 (for fast driving).

TANK CAPACITY: 12 Imperial gallons.
Oil sump, 12 pints.
Cooling system, 20 pints (plus 1 pint if heater is fitted).

TURNING CIRCLE: 35ft 0in (L and R).
Steering wheel turns (lock to lock): 2¾.

DIMENSIONS: Wheelbase: 7ft 8in.
Track: F, 4ft 0¾in; R, 4ft 2in.
Length (overall): 13ft 1½in.
Height: 4ft 1in.
Width: 5ft 0½in.
Ground clearance: 5½in.
Frontal area: 16.6 sq ft (approximately) with hood up.

ELECTRICAL SYSTEM: 12-volt; 51 ampère-hour battery.
Head lights: Double dip; 42—36 watt bulbs.

SUSPENSION: Front, independent with coil springs and wishbones, anti-roll bar. Rear, half-elliptic leaf springs and Panhard rod.

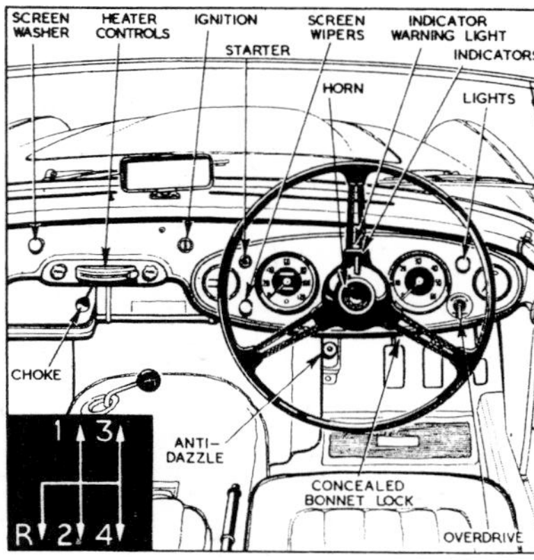
SCREEN WASHER
HEATER CONTROLS
IGNITION
SCREEN WIPERS
INDICATOR WARNING LIGHT
STARTER
INDICATORS
HORN
LIGHTS
CHOKE
ANTI-DAZZLE
CONCEALED BONNET LOCK
OVERDRIVE
1 3
R 2 4

THE AUTOCAR, 2 NOVEMBER 1956

AUSTIN-HEALEY 100 SIX . . .

Visibility with the hood up is excellent, but the height of the rear view mirror above the scuttle is insufficient to make full use of the large rear window panel. One is not conscious of any draughts in the car when closed; in fact, after some miles of fast driving, the cockpit is apt to become rather too warm, even when the fresh-air intake is opened. The two rear seats are suitable for small children, and it is possible for an adult to sit across the car. He would, however, find his head well above the windscreen level, and with the hood erect would be unable to sit upright.

Provision of these seats has restricted the volume of the luggage locker, which now also houses the spare wheel and battery, and it is virtually impossible to stow even a small suitcase. The wisdom of placing the battery there also seems questionable. The occasional seats, moreover, have a central hump which likewise prevents a suitcase from fitting there, and this lack of properly shaped luggage accommodation might prove a severe handicap for the many who will be driving their Austin-Healeys on trans-Continental marathons. Such inadequacy of baggage space calls for the use of an external rack, but a more satisfactory solution might be to arrange external stowage of the spare wheel when it is necessary to carry extra luggage.

Stowage for small articles in the cockpit is provided by a deep pocket in each door and a shelf below the left side of the facia panel. Part of this shelf is, somewhat un-expectedly, occupied by the screen-wash bottle. Locking of the doors is rather awkward, for the left door locks with the ignition key, and the right by means of a small interior catch. It would be better if this arrangement were reversed, or if both doors could be locked by the key, since it is none too easy for the driver to move over the central gear box hump and handbrake.

The instrument panel is well laid out, and the dials easily read and well lit. There is no rheostat switch, but the lighting is not strong enough to annoy the driver, nor is there any reflection in the windscreen. In full ahead and dipped positions the head lamps earn good marks, and the twin high-frequency horns have powerful notes. The windscreen wipers are efficient, and clear a reasonable area of the screen. The ribbed tonneau cover is exceptionally neat, and can be used with the driver only in the car. An improved feature is that the fuel tank filler is now on the outside of the body rather than inside the locker, and that it can take the full flow from a garage pump; the cap, however, proved difficult to release or replace.

The Austin-Healey 100 Six is fast, safe, efficient and easy to drive. It is equally well suited to the elderly owner who has no intention of travelling at 100 m.p.h., but enjoys driving for its own sake and prefers it with a breath of fresh air, and to the younger sportsman to whom speed and acceleration mean almost everything. Any who seek even more performance than the car offers in standard form will know that the engine has a considerable untapped reserve, and that the car as a whole is exceptionally tough.

Autocar road test 1978

Austin-Healey 3000 Mk. III CONVERTIBLE 2,912 c.c.

SUN-CAPPED Dolomites and the distant roar and squeal of one of the works rally cars scrambling its way up the Gavia pass—this perhaps is the image that some people have of the big Austin-Healey at work. But there is a world of difference between those frequent winners, the former Spartan works rally cars, and the over-the-counter product of today—the 3000 Mk. III

For as long as many of us care to remember there has been a big Healey in the price lists. The car has been through several variations of engine size, but now, like an ageing but still beautiful dowager, repeated face lifts can no longer wholly hide the ravages of time and progress.

For many years a change in the model of the Healey has been marked with either the subtraction or addition of a carburettor; however, the Mk. III continues with two S.U. carburettors for the Series C 2,912 c.c. engine, with diameter increased by 0·25in. to 2in. With the new carburettors and a camshaft of improved design the power output of the engine has been raised from 137 b.h.p. at 4,750 r.p.m. to 148 b.h.p. at 5,250 r.p.m. Although this comparatively unsophisticated six-cylinder engine must now be very near the end of its development, it seems to have gained in flexibility and is virtually free from any temperament.

Provided full use is made of the choke, starting from cold is good. The engine takes a long time to warm through and

spits back through the carburettors if pushed at all hard before it is warm. The all-too-frequent trouble of running-on still persists and could only be prevented by opening the throttles wide as the ignition was switched off.

Although the big Healey has never been a noisy car in standard form, the latest design of exhaust system, with two silencers on the left side of the car and a further two set transversely under the boot floor, cuts the noise down to almost saloon car level at anything but near-peak engine

PRICES		£	s	d
Sports Convertible		915	0	0
Purchase tax		191	3	9
	Total (in G.B.)	1,106	3	9
Extras (including P.T.)				
Overdrive		60	8	4
Wire wheels		30	4	2
Fresh air heater		18	14	7
Telescopic steering column		2	8	4
Seat belts (each)		5	5	0

How the Austin-Healey 3000 Mk. III compares:

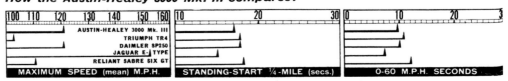

Super Profile

Autocar road test • No. 1978

Make • AUSTIN-HEALEY   Type • 3000 Mk. III (2,912 c.c.)
(Front engine, rear-wheel drive)

Manufacturers : Austin Motor Co. Ltd., Longbridge, Birmingham

Test Conditions
Weather ... Dry and sunny with 0-5 m.p.h. wind
Temperature .... 9 deg. C. (48 deg. F.)
Barometer .... 29.6in. Hg.
Dry concrete and tarmac surfaces.

Weight
Kerb weight (with oil, water and half-full fuel tank)
23.5 cwt (2,604lb-1,180kg)
Front-rear distribution, per cent F, 52; R, 48
Laden as tested ......26.5 cwt (2,940lb-1,333kg)

Turning Circles
Between kerbs ...... L, 35ft 0in.; R, 34ft 10in.
Between walls ...... L, 36ft 3in.; R, 35ft 10in.
Turns of steering wheel lock to lock 3

FUEL AND OIL CONSUMPTION

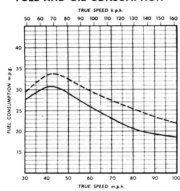

FUEL ....Super premium grade
(101 octane RM)

Test Distance ....1,583 miles

Overall Consumption ...... 20.3 m.p.g.
(13.9 litres/100 km.)

Estimated Consumption (DIN) 24.9 m.p.g.
(11.4 litres/100 km.)

OIL: SAE 10W30 ... Consumption 1,600 m.p.g.

HILL CLIMBING AT STEADY SPEEDS

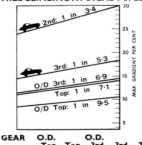

2nd: 1 in 3.4
3rd: 1 in 5.3
O/D 3rd: 1 in 6.9
Top: 1 in 7.1
O/D Top: 1 in 9.5

GEAR	O.D. Top	Top	O.D. 3rd	3rd	2nd
PULL (lb per ton)	235	310	340	410	635

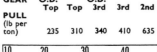

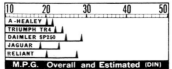

M.P.G. Overall and Estimated (DIN)

MAXIMUM SPEEDS AND ACCELERATION TIMES

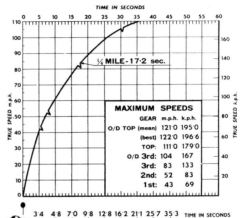

¼ MILE - 17.2 sec.

MAXIMUM SPEEDS		
GEAR	m.p.h.	k.p.h.
O/D TOP (mean)	121.0	195.0
(best)	122.0	196.6
TOP:	111.0	179.0
O/D 3rd:	104	167
3rd:	83	133
2nd:	52	83
1st:	43	69

TIME IN SECONDS									
	3.4	4.8	7.0	9.8	12.8	16.2	21.1	25.7	35.3
TRUE SPEED m.p.h.	0	30	40	50	60	70	80	90	100 100
CAR SPEEDOMETER		28	40	48	58	70	80	93	104 114

Speed range, gear ratios and time in seconds

m.p.h.	O.D. Top (3.14)	Top (3.91)	O.Third (4.74)	Third (5.12)	Second (8.05)	First (11.26)
10—30	—	—	—	6.1	4.2	3.0
20—40	—	7.5	6.6	4.1	3.2	2.8
30—50	9.3	6.8	6.3	5.4	3.4	—
40—60	8.7	6.9	6.8	4.9	—	—
50—70	10.7	7.9	7.3	5.5	—	—
60—80	12.1	8.1	7.8	6.4	—	—
70—90	13.6	9.0	8.2	—	—	—
80—100	15.7	9.9	9.0	—	—	—
90—110	18.2	14.2	—	—	—	—

BRAKES
(from 30 m.p.h. in neutral)

Pedal load	Retardation	Equiv. distance
25lb	0.23g	131ft
50lb	0.72g	42ft
75lb	0.81g	37ft
100lb	0.92g	32.8ft
Handbrake	0.37g	81ft

CLUTCH
Pedal load and travel—40lb and 6in.

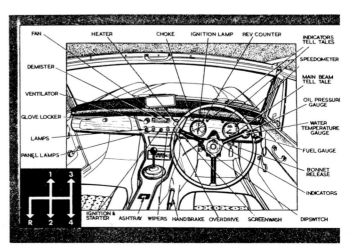

FAN · HEATER · CHOKE · IGNITION LAMP · REV COUNTER · INDICATORS TELL TALES · SPEEDOMETER · MAIN BEAM TELL TALE · OIL PRESSURE GAUGE · WATER TEMPERATURE GAUGE · FUEL GAUGE · BONNET RELEASE · INDICATORS · DIPSWITCH · SCREENWASH · OVERDRIVE · HANDBRAKE · WIPERS · ASHTRAY · IGNITION & STARTER · PANEL LAMPS · LAMPS · GLOVE LOCKER · VENTILATOR · DEMISTER

AUTOCAR, 12 June 1964

Austin-Healey 3000 Mk. III

A central console, wood-trimmed facia and re-grouped instruments are new to the model; fixed quarter-light frames on the front doors can be too close to the occupants' head when getting in

revs. However, the car still suffers from very limited ground clearance and over rough roads one has to put up with bangs and thumps when the silencers touch bumps on the surface.

The test car was fitted with the optional extra Laycock de Normanville overdrive, working on third and top gears. With overdrive, a lower back axle ratio is used—3·91 in place of the normal 3·55 to 1 ratio. While this does make the car extremely flexible in the upper ratios at low engine revs, it tends to emphasize the large gap between second and third gears, with their respective maximum speeds of 52 and 83 m.p.h. Overdrive third gear produced a maximum of 104 m.p.h., direct top 111 m.p.h. and overdrive top gave a mean maximum speed of 121 m.p.h. Overdrive, operated by a switch on the facia, engages very smoothly indeed; to return to direct drive the engine has to be pulling before an inhibitor switch will release the overdrive. This prevents jolts in the transmission.

In practice, very high averages can be maintained on main roads by using just direct and overdrive top gears, the car wafting along at around the 90 mark with no more than 4,000 r.p.m. on the rev counter.

The big Healey's take-off from standstill is impressive. Without tyre squeal or wheel-spin, it reached 30 m.p.h. in 3·4 40 in 4·8, 60 in 9·8 and 100 in 25·7sec. At maximum revs—5,250 r.p.m. in this case—the combined noise of

engine, cooling fan, unsilenced carburettor air intakes and exhaust reaches almost Grand Prix levels and on the maximum speed runs the scream of wind round the windows and hood adds to the din. Prolonged motorway driving at very high speeds becomes tiring for this reason.

Clutch Improved

Later models of the Austin-Healey 3000 Mk. II were fitted with diaphragm spring clutches but this was the first model of the make we have been able to drive fitted with one. The pressure is light—only 40lb—and the length of travel and smoothness of engagement are more like those of a touring car than a 120 m.p.h. sports car. Effective, rather heavy synchromesh makes gear-changing a bit slow on the upper three ratios and it is almost impossible to get into first gear while on the move without crunching. The position of the gear lever is such that one has to use a cranked elbow action to make changes, but this soon becomes quite a natural movement.

The years of competition and development have certainly improved the car's handling. For normal motoring, the car has slight understeer, but when time is short, the right foot can turn this into an accurately controllable power oversteer. When cornering hard the driver has to beware of

Left: The back of the rear seat folds forward to make a good luggage platform—which is needed as the boot (right) is much taken up by spare wheel, battery and hood covers

The unmistakable lines of the big Healey still suggest potency. The small upper rear "lamps" are reflectors

bumps in the road, which can throw the car off course with unexpected force. In the wet, an unwary jab on the accelerator can bring the tail of the car skating round and a good deal of caution has to be used on corners.

We were unable to test the car's handling on our special *pavé* track for fear of wiping off the exhaust system, but on a rough side road, the short suspension movements and firm damping make the car twitch about unless the driver concentrates on holding direction. The steering itself is heavy at low speeds, but once the car gets on to the open road it becomes a good deal lighter. At near-maximum speed, the car controls very well and holds a straight course.

Although a vacuum servo is standard equipment on the Mk. III models—it was an extra on the previous model—the brakes still feel heavy, but they are very powerful. Heavy braking from high speeds is accompanied by slight weaving; this never builds up to anything near dangerous proportions, but is nevertheless disconcerting. The pull-up handbrake, located between the driving seat and transmission tunnel held the car easily on a 1-in-3 hill, from where take-off was of the "rocket" variety, with spinning wheels.

Driving Position

In its appointments the Austin-Healey 3000 Mk. III is now more of a touring car than a sports car. The new panel design and the trim are attractive, almost luxurious. In these days of straight-arm steering, the driver of the big Healey has to get used to the old Vintage bent arm position again, with the huge 17in. diameter steering wheel only a matter of inches from his chest. On the test car the telescopic steering column (an extra) was fitted. If it had put the wheel 3in *nearer* the facia it would have been more help. The pedals are small and set close together. If space and layout allowed the pedal group to be brought back three inches and the seat moved back a similar distance, the driving position would be far more comfortable. The seats are rather small and hard, with cushions that "set" after a few miles. At the end of a long drive you are glad to have a good stretch to restore the circulation.

The "traditional" British love of wood has extended to this Healey and the dashboard has walnut veneer on its two outer panels. The centre of the facia now extends downwards to form a central console with the deep transmission tunnel. There are spaces in this console for a radio and loudspeaker.

A comprehensive set of instruments is grouped behind the steering wheel and comprises a speedometer, with total and trip mileage recorders, rev counter, combined oil pressure and water temperature gauge and fuel gauge. While driving, this last instrument swings freely between full and empty as soon as the tank contents have dropped to about

three-quarters full. In the centre of the facia are four identical switches in pairs on each side of the ignition-starter switch; they control driving and panel lamps, and screenwipers and overdrive. A differently shaped toggle for the O.D. switch would make it more easily identifiable; at

Not a spare inch is wasted under the bonnet; the lid still has to be propped open with a stay

night it is easy to flick the wrong switch and start the single speed wipers working instead of selecting overdrive. A single quadrant control adjusts the temperature of the heater, distribution of flow between the car and windscreen being adjusted by two flaps set high under the back of the dashboard.

There is a large lockable cubby in the facia and a non-locking glove box on the transmission tunnel, with a padded top to form an armrest for driver or passenger. Two small seats for children are fitted in the back, and an adult, sitting sideways, could be packed in for short trips. The backrest of this seat folds forward and is held by two substantial bolts to form a large luggage platform, with a lip on the leading edge to prevent suitcases sliding forward. This platform is really valuable because the boot is mainly occupied by the spare wheel and battery and can hold only one small grip and some odds and ends. Now that winding windows are fitted and a hardtop is offered, B.M.C. ought to provide locks for the doors. They do provide a battery master switch in the boot which cuts off all current—including the side lamps for parking at night. A prop rod has to be slotted into a catch to hold the boot open.

In these days of international conformity over direction indicators, the big Healey still uses the side and tail lamps as indicators and at night they can be confusing to following traffic if one is braking and indicating at the same time. Twin horns with an impressive volume are fitted.

The well-fitting hood was rain-tight and did not flap at high speeds; it is held down on to the screen rail by two

over-centre clips with ominously sharp projections. The convertible type hood can be folded back easily and in a matter of seconds, and a hood cover is provided. Fresh-air ventilation can be greatly increased in warm weather by un-zipping the whole of the back window and folding it down. In summer, the car still suffers from too much heat coming through from the engine and to help overcome this a cold air vent is fitted under the dash—on the left-hand side.

This car is much faster than the Mk. II version, and is more economical, averaging 20·3 m.p.g. overall. Commuting and a series of fast, short runs, where maximum revs were frequently being used, dropped the consumption to 18·7 m.p.g.; on everyday motoring, the fuel consumption is around the 22 m.p.g. mark. The 12-gallon fuel tank filled easily, without any blow back. During the 1,583 miles of testing eight pints of oil were used, but the car had been fitted with new piston rings shortly before it was handed over for test and probably they were still bedding-in.

Under the bonnet, the husky six-cylinder engine fills every inch of available space, with wires and cables running everywhere. The screenwasher bottle, which used to be inside the passenger cockpit, has now been moved under the bonnet. The lid is held shut by two safety catches and is held open with a stay.

Despite some dated features, the big Healey is still terrific fun to drive. Tractable, capable of an immense amount of hard work with reasonable economy, it will still have its devotees long after production has ceased.

Specification: Austin-Healey 3000 Mk. III Convertible

PERFORMANCE DATA
Overdrive top gear m.p.h. per 1,000 r.p.m. ...	23·0
Top gear m.p.h. per 1,000 r.p.m.	18·9
Mean piston speed at max. power........	3,035ft/min.
Engine revs. at mean max. speed	5,260 r.p.m.
B.h.p. per ton laden	111·2

▼ **Scale: 0.3in. to 1ft. Cushions uncompressed.**

ENGINE
Cylinders ...	... 6-in-line
Bore ...	... 83·4mm (3·28in.)
Stroke ...	... 88·9mm (3·50in.)
Displacement	... 2,912 c.c. (178 cu. in.)
Valve gear ...	... Overhead, pushrods and rockers
Compression ratio	9·0-to-1
Carburettors ...	2 S.U. HD8
Fuel pump ...	... S.U. electric
Oil filter ...	... Full flow, renewable element
Max. power ...	148 b.h.p. (net) at 5,250 r.p.m.
Max. torque ...	165·2 lb. ft. at 3,500 r.p.m.

TRANSMISSION
Clutch ...	Borg and Beck diaphragm spring, 9·5in. dia.
Gearbox ...	Four speed, synchromesh on 2nd, 3rd and Top; central control
Overall ratios	O.D. Top 0·82, Top 1·00; O.D. Third 1·08, Third 1·31, Second 2·06; First 2·88; Reverse 3·72
Final drive ...	Hypoid bevel, 3·91

CHASSIS
Construction	Boxed cruciform chassis, with steel and aluminium body

SUSPENSION
Front ...	Independent, coil springs and wishbones, lever arm dampers, anti-roll bar
Rear ...	Live axle, half elliptic leaf springs, Panhard rod, lever arm dampers
Steering ...	Cam and peg
Wheel dia. ...	17in.

BRAKES
Type ...	Girling hydraulic, disc front drum rear, vacuum servo
Dimensions	F, 11·25in. dia. R, 11·0in. dia., 2·25in. wide shoes
Swept area	F, 228 sq. in.; R, 155·5 sq. in. Total: 383·5 sq. in. (286 sq. in. per ton laden)

WHEELS
Type ...	Pressed steel disc standard, wire-spoked, centre-lock extra, 4·5in. wide rim
Tyres ...	5·90—15in. Dunlop RS5 with tubes

EQUIPMENT
Battery ...	12-volt 57-amp. hr.
Headlamps ...	36-48 watt
Reversing lamp ...	None
Electric fuses ...	2
Screen wipers ...	2, single speed, self parking
Screen washer ...	Standard, manual plunger
Interior heater ...	Extra, fresh air, electric booster
Safety belts ...	Extra, anchorages provided
Interior trim ...	Ambla leathercloth
Floor covering ...	Carpet
Starting handle ...	No provision
Jack ...	Screw type
Jacking points ...	4, on suspension
Other bodies ...	None

MAINTENANCE
Fuel tank ...	12 Imp. gallons (no reserve)
Cooling system ...	20 pints (including heater)
Engine sump ...	12·75 pints SAE 10W30. Change oil every 3,000 miles; change filter element every 6,000 miles
Gearbox and overdrive ...	7 pints SAE 30. Change oil every 6,000 miles
Final drive ...	3 pints SAE 90EP. Change oil every 6,000 miles
Grease ...	11 points every 3,000 miles
Tyre pressures ...	F, 20; R, 25 p.s.i. (normal driving). F, 25; R, 30 p.s.i. (fast driving)

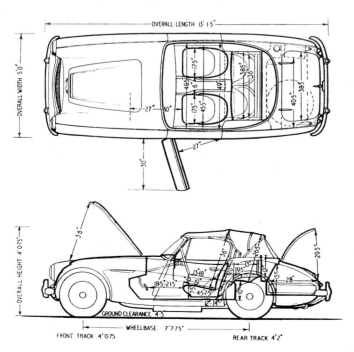

OVERALL LENGTH 13' 1·5"
OVERALL WIDTH 5'0"
OVERALL HEIGHT 4'0·75"
GROUND CLEARANCE 4·5"
WHEELBASE 7'7·75"
FRONT TRACK 4'0·75"
REAR TRACK 4'2"

Owner's View

Although the Austin-Healey has been exported to very many markets, some quite small, the greatest volume by far went to North America. Indeed, the British sports car enthusiast should realise that without the sales volume presented by this market there would not have been Austin-Healeys, MGs, Jaguars and TRs for them to buy. It was only this huge American volume which justified the design effort and investment in manufacturing facilities for the production of what were fairly specialist cars. In order to obtain an insight into what attributes of British sports cars attract American enthusiasts to the Austin-Healey models I sought the views of an active owner in that country and contrasted them with those of a similar UK owner.

Dave Ramstad is an Avionics Designer with a major US aircraft manufacturer and drives a 2.8 litre Ford Capri for every day use having previously used a Firebird Trans-Am, so he is clearly performance orientated! Keith Clapham is a UK company director and owns several interesting cars. He drives a Volvo Turbo for daily use when not using his BJ8.

To begin, I asked both men what it was that first attracted them to the Big Healey. For Dave, it was a life long fascination for all things automotive which focused down through European cars in general, then British Sports cars and finally and clearly onto the Big Healey which was reaching the United States in large numbers just at the time he became a licensed driver for the first time. Driving a friend's BN1 introduced Dave to the world of Healeys, but it was 1962 before he was able to purchase his first example, a red over black BN4. Keith's introduction was quite different. As a small boy he lived near to the Austin plant at Longbridge and was quite used to seeing transporter vehicles loaded with cars passing his home, and did not take too much notice of this traffic until one day his attention was caught by a load of very good looking soft top cars. He discovered later that these were Austin-Healey 100s and he was captured! But it was not until 1976 when a visiting friend arrived in a 3000 Mk III and took him for a drive that the school boy memories came flooding back, bringing with them a burning desire to own a Healey. Keith's first Austin Healey was a "100" restoration job, but this had to be abandoned and sold in 1979 due to lack of time resulting from the pressure of business life. It was in 1981 that he obtained a very presentable 1966 BJ8, a car which he still owns. This car had had only three previous owners and was purchased from a club member who had done much work to bring it up to a good reliable condition.

Dave's first Healey was written off by an overzealous friend in 1965 whilst he was away serving in the United States Navy and was replaced in the Autumn of 1966 by a white, late series 100-6 which served him well, taking in a 3800 miles trans-America house move to Florida. This car firmly cemented the Healey bond and remained with Dave until traded-in for his present BJ8.

Although Keith's car was in good order, his first Concours d'Elegance attempt showed that some attention was required if he was to have the car he really wanted. After going the rounds of the rebuild specialists he realised that a high cost and long time off the road was to be expected and so decided he would do the work himself. Working to a plan, the chassis, floors, boot area, and interior trim were completed during the first winter. Mechanical parts overhaul took up the second winter with the third winter being given over to exterior trim, body paint and hood. This was all accomplished with the help of his wife and Keith Boyer of K & JB Restorations. The result has been a prize winning car at the Northern Centre "Lakes Weekend" in May 1986.

As Dave's two BN4 cars had much unknown history before his ownership, they both exhibited many of the familiar Healey problems! These were fixed by Dave as and when resources permitted and provided reliable and enjoyable motoring. His present car is his third Big Healey and was purchased new in mid 1967. This has enabled Dave to give the car the care and attention necessary to keep the car in first class condition, and it has responded by being utterly reliable and trouble free. After 80,000 miles the power unit has not been opened up and Dave's simple advice to any owner wishing to obtain the same service from their Healey is to stay on top of periodic maintenance, adjustment and cleaning.

Whilst rebuilding his car, Keith took the opportunity to embody some proven performance improvement changes. The cylinder head was gas-flowed and a higher lift camshaft was installed. The crankshaft was tuftrided, the flywheel lightened and the whole engine assembly was balanced. Dampers were uprated by 50% and a one inch diameter front anti-roll bar was fitted. To go with all these changes a 3.5:1 final drive unit from a non-overdrive car was substituted for the 3.9:1 ratio standard for overdrive cars already fitted. The effect has been to produce a 130+ mph car which will return between 22 and 24 mpg, a very significant improvement over the standard BJ8.

Because he started with a complete car, Keith has not experienced any serious spare parts problems, but mentioned A-H, Spares and SC Austin-Healey Parts as both being very helpful when the requirement for a part arose. Dave made the point that because he has owned his car from new he can not be regarded as having a wholly representative view of the spare parts market, but offers the comment that the growth of the old car hobby in general and interest in the Austin-Healey in particular has led to a steady growth of specialist firms since the early 1970's and he believes that one should not anticipate any serious problems in the forseeable future. In fact the dilemma today has become one of sorting out the specialists to find the one that best suits the individual owner.

When asked about performance, both Dave and Keith said that this was "exciting". Dave endorsed his response by adding that every Austin-Healey he has owned with the possible exception of the 1957 102 bhp 100-6 had offered more performance and handling capability than he could fully utilize. The surge from rest to 60mph in under ten seconds, relaxed all day cruising at 70 to 90mph with a top speed of 120 mph are more than adequate for the sporting motorist.

Both of Dave's earlier 100-6 cars were in daily year round service as was his present 3000 Mk III for the first five years of his ownership. This car took Dave and his wife on honeymoon in 1968 and brought their first child home

in 1970 and except for obvious space limitations common to all Sports Cars was just as practical and reliable for everyday use as a common family sedan. Because the mechanical components are based on volume built family cars, this reliability when coupled with regular maintenance should perhaps not be too suprising. However, because no more Austin-Healeys will ever be built again, Dave in common with most owners does not these days care to subject his car to daily use, preferring to keep it for rather more special events such as shows and club meetings. Keith keeps his car insured and taxed for road use all the year round and uses it regularly for business trips when the carriage of goods and samples is not necessary. He finds it a thoroughly practical car for this purpose whenever possible. Running costs are less than for his Volvo and has the added advantage of being a vehicle which is increasing in value! Whenever possible even in wet weather, Keith runs with the hood down.

Both owners have entered their cars in Show Competition and whilst Keith's is still up to a first class standard, Dave's unrestored and 100% original machine does now suffer some cosmetic deterioration of its metallic golden beige body paint and so is temporarily retired from these activities. It will return! Neither owner subjects his car to hard driving competitive events over poor or indifferent surfaces, nor to racing. Although these types of events are offered in the U.K., they appear not to be encouraged in the USA as they are not thought to be suitable for ageing motor cars of increasing value.

In the UK and the United States there are flourishing owners' Clubs and both Keith and Dave are members of their local

area groups. Keith believes that anyone contemplating buying an Austin-Healey should join their nearest club, go along to meetings and talk to owners who will know all the problems to be anticipated. They may also have that vital spare part sought to complete a repair or restoration. Dave would also encourage any enthusiast to become involved with their local club. He feels that membership bringing with it social activities, technical sessions, and magazines containing historical studies and technical articles is of invaluable benefit to all owners. Keith also mentioned the attraction of the U.K. Clubs specialist Insurance Broker and found this of great help in holding down running costs.

Both agreed that they derive much pleasure from owning a car which combines beauty, performance, strength, ease and low cost maintenance which has become an appreciating asset. This combination of virtues has not been matched by any other sports car to this very day.

In conclusion Keith and Dave were asked what advice they would give to potential Big Healey owners. Dave said that they should thoroughly research the marque and talk to several owners, because this hard riding muscular sports car is not for everyone. Having satisfied oneself that this is the car to own, be careful in choosing one. Be sure that it can be brought up to the standard required and that personal commitment and resources are adequate for the task. Be prepared to give it a great deal of tender loving care! Keith was emphatic in saying that one should buy today if possible and enjoy it now, as tomorrow the purchase price will be higher. The only new Big Healeys now are rebuilt ones and there is a finite number of these!

BUYING

Buying

It is now nearly twenty years since the production of the Big Healey ended in December 1967, so that almost any car being offered for sale will have run a substantial mileage and suffered to some extent from the wear and corrosion problems which beset all Austin-Healey cars. Of course, there are a few examples which have been very carefully looked after by the only one owner, and which will have recorded quite a low mileage, but these are very much the exception and a potential buyer will be very lucky to find such a car. With the rising interest in classic British sports cars and the increasing notional values which follow, there is a growing number of restored cars coming onto the market as well as a surprising number of total rebuild project cars. Consequently the aspiring owner is faced with the choice of several options conditioned by what he can afford.

The worth of a car is on one hand the price the vendor expects to obtain for it and on the other hand it is the price a purchaser is willing to pay, so that it is quite impossible to quote specific guidelines. Many vendors appear to be of the opinion because after restoration a car may have quite a substantical value, they are as of right, entitled to receive some of that value before it accrues! Buyers should resist this attitude and if possessed of sufficient will power, turn away from the temptingly easy project before them and look elsewhere. Restoration is neither cheap nor easy, and potential owners should be quite clear in their own minds what they expect of their cars and their capabilities of achieving this, before embarking on an adventure which could turn out to be both expensive and demoralising.

Frequently offered for sale are cars which have had much time and money expended upon them, both of which have been exhausted before the project has come to fruition. In these cases the vendor will invariably pitch the asking price to cover all the outstanding costs in the belief that this is reasonable and justifiable, which it is not since the standard of the work carried out may not be up to that demanded by the purchaser's requirements. Many prospective purchasers cherish the idea of owning a 100 points condition car without appreciating the high costs involved in achieving this objective, quite failing to realise that total restoration costs to achieve such a standard can exceed the market value of the finished car.

For the enthusiast who is determined to own a first class car, the choice comes down to either buying a car which has been fully restored to known and approved standards, usually by a recognised specialist, or buying a vehicle in need of total restoration and then spending a great deal of money with a specialist restoration business. Alternatively, if possessed of adequate skill and determination, owners can do much of the work themselves to hold down costs, but some tasks, especially finish painting the body will best be carried out by experts. If the restoration route is chosen the buyer should pay the lowest possible price for the base vehicle. This may appear to be stating the obvious, but there is no point in spending a large sum of money on what amounts in fact to a license to spend a great deal more money. Several cars should be looked at before making a choice and hasty decisions should be resisted because ill considered actions can often result in much anguish later on when the magnitude of the task ahead is revealed.

Equally, there is no point in paying quite a large sum for what appears to be an 80 points car in the belief that a modest further outlay will bring it up to 100 points standard. The new owner will almost certainly end up totally rebuilding the car at enormous cost as the various and inevitable shortcomings are exposed during the first weeks and months of ownership. This reinforces the caveat that prospective owners should be clear as to what they want from their cars. Do they want to participate in Concours d'Elegance competitions, or will they be satisfied with a good and reliable car that they enjoy at a practical level without worrying about small details of specification and presentation? Reconciling their requirements with their means and capabilities will avoid much distress at a later stage. In any event, it should be appreciated that the purchase, restoration and ownership of a Big Healey is not a venture to be undertaken by the financially faint hearted, but because values of high quality cars will at least be maintained at current levels as demand for the remaining examples is sustained, the investment can be considered sound.

If there are no financial constraints and the buyer chooses to purchase a top class car, then it is only necessary to check on where the restoration work was done, to be reasonably satisfied as to the quality of the vehicle, although it is always a worthwhile safeguard to seek the opinion of an independent expert because sometimes, either as a matter of expediency or necessity, some deviation from correct original specification may have been introduced.

If seeking a car for restoration, there are many problem areas to check out, some safety-critical and some specification related. Because of the age of the cars, and especially in the case of the 100-6, early examples of which are now thirty years old, many will have been modified or "improved" by the replacement of correct specification parts with non-original parts when the original part suffered damage or not easily repaired wear and tear. If any correct specification detail parts are missing then this should be used as a bargaining counter when agreeing a price.

When the Austin-Healey was designed, the effects of built-in mud traps were not understood and as a consequence the whole of the car is extremely vulnerable to rust attack. Unless the car has been rebuilt or run for only a very low mileage with careful garaging, the outer body skin panels are certain to be effected to a greater or lesser extent by rust and in some cases may have been replaced by glass fibre reproduction panels. Although these have a good appearance, they will certainly diminish the value of the car. Where the original steel wing panels remain on the car they will invariably be rusting along their lower edges and at the return flanges at front and rear door shut pillars which themselves will also be showing signs of severe attack, even if concealed behind trim cover plates. Sill sections at the point where the wings attach, and also below the doors, will also be affected by corrosion damage, possibly extending in to the floor panels. Replacement steel panels

for all affected areas are now available from specialist suppliers, but in some cases it will be preferable to repair front wings in order to preserve a good fit which is critical to appearance.

Front and rear body centre sections shroud panels are pressed from aluminium and in old cars could be exhibiting fatigue cracks at the corner radii of bonnet and boot lid openings. They are also liable to suffer electrolytic corrosion along the outer edge flanges where the wing panels bolt up to them.

Although these problems can be rectified by a skilled body repair man, particular attention should be paid to the examination of the shroud panels to check for accident damage which can be very difficult to repair and reshape to a satisfactory standard. Replacement shrouds are not available as a complete assembly, although repair sections can now be obtained from specialist parts suppliers, but the condition of these large body panels is a critical factor in the choice of a car.

Although of robust design, the Healey chassis frame is susceptible to both rust attack and accident damage. The side members should be straight and parallel from front to rear with no evidence of bending as the result of a front end collision. Front corner impacts will usually push the top suspension tower backwards and the lower rear wishbone arm inwards to produce a nasty dog-leg bend in the chassis side rail, extending as far back as the toe box floor panel. A severe kerb strike on a front wheel can produce similar damage to a lesser degree.

Because the front damper attachment screws tend to work loose, the captive nuts in the mounting platform are liable to fretting and eventual stripping. In extreme cases, the plate itself can tear out. Fortunately, replacement plates are now available to solve what was a difficult repair

problem. Invariably the bottom face of the front cross member will be damaged where thoughtless owners have jacked up the very heavy front end of the car without placing a bearer between the jack pad and the member. Sometimes the damage from these sections combined with rusting can be so severe as to leave large holes in this area.

Chassis side outriggers supporting the floors and sill panels are also liable to rusting, especially at the rear where there is less protection from the oil film blown back from the engine bay. Of particular importance in this area are the rear spring shackle mountings on the rear outriggers, since these can tear away under load if seriously weakened by rust. The rear shackle pins can seize in their bushes if routine greasing has been neglected which regretably is often the case when a car has had many owners. The rear cross member is also liable to jacking damage and frequently suffers from rust damage because it receives little or no protection from under body oil film blow back.

Rear damper mounting plates should be examined at their attachment to the chassis because the longitudinal twisting stresses set up by the resistive action of the dampers tend to cause cracks to develop in the sides of the chassis rails. Simple welding can effect a cure to this problem.

Great care should be directed towards chassis examination since an apparently sound frame can be suffering from unseen internal corrosion of the members. Fortunately repair sections covering most problem areas are now available from the specialists so that the essential structural integrity of chassis may be restored.

The major mechanical assemblies are robust, reliable and easily rebuilt, although costs for this work can absorb a great deal of money especially if wear has been serious. The six cylinder "C" series BMC engine is a rugged unit capable of absorbing much abuse, but should be checked for excessive wear. In particular, the crankcase ventilation system should be operative otherwise high oil consumption will result. Oil pressure should be at least 50 psi when running, with a minimum 20 psi at hot idle, and whilst a very small amount of blue smoke from the exhaust tail pipe may be acceptable, there should be no evidence in the engine compartment of the typically sickly sweet smell of piston ring blow-by, after returning from a trial run in the car.

Although gearbox synchromesh may not be up to modern car standards, the box should not be particularly noisy and should not jump out of gear either on the over-run or on drive under power. For later cars, replacement gear sets are now available, but faulty gearboxes remain a very expensive unit to overhaul. Where fitted, the Laycock overdrive unit is usually very reliable, unless allowed to run with insufficient oil. Rebuilding of these units by specialists is straightforward but expensive.

Rear axles are very strong and generally trouble free, but the splined hub extensions should be checked for corrosion and fretting wear resulting from inadequate greasing and running with improperly tightened knock-off hub nuts. Damage to these parts could lead to the loss of a rear wheel with very serious consequences. Wheels will invariably have broken and loose spokes, and may have worn internal splines for the same reasons that the hub extensions will be showing signs of damage. Wheel problems are most easily dealt with by straight exchange from specialist suppliers although in the U.K. it is possible, if preferred, to have wheels rebuilt by a diminishing number of wheelwrights. This is an option not generally available to overseas owners and is responsible for some US owners preferring the basic steel disc wheel of the standard specification.

On a car which has covered many thousands of miles in the hands of several owners some of which may have been less than prudent in their attention to routine maintenance tasks, the front suspension will undoubtedly be showing signs of serious wear, especially at the lower wishbone arm outer end fulcrum pins. It is essential to the inherently good handling characteristics of the car and indeed to its safety, that the front suspension and steering system is in first class order. The difference in feel between a "loose" car and one that has a properly set up suspension is quite dramatic. Great care and attention should be paid to ensuring that all suspension and brake system parts are renewed to new car condition in view of the front end weight and high performance potential of six cylinder Austin Healey models. The need to have a twenty to thirty years old, obviously fast and attractive looking car in first class mechanical condition can not be over emphasised if the hostility of the authorities is not to be aroused in the unfortunate event of either some mishap occuring or an infringement of the traffic laws relating to speed limits. Since all parts necessary to achieve a well set up car are readily available from many sources, there is no excuse for not having the car in a safe and fully roadworthy condition.

Electrical systems are straightforward but may require re-wiring in parts as the original cotton braiding on the harness may have rotted away and the bullet connectors badly corroded leading to dead circuits. Beware of a car festooned with wires taped to the original harness and other underbonnet parts! First class reproduction harnesses are now available to remedy electrical problems.

By now it will be realised that ownership of a Big Healey at whatever standard required is entirely feasible since rebuilding of almost any car is restricted only by the financial resources and degree of commitment of the owner. Indeed, it is interesting to note that cars until recently regarded as only suitable for breaking-up for spares are now being dragged back from the grave for rebuilding such is the continuing demand for Austin-Healeys of all description and type. This demand is reflected in the increasing attention being paid to the early 100-6 models which were always very much in the shadow of the better 3000 variants. None the less, the 3000 and especially the later Convertible derivatives remain the most sought after Big Healeys and will undoubtedly remain so. Their performance and creature comforts make them an entirely practical everyday car should this be necessary, but buyers should not expect them to be directly comparable with current production cars when used for this purpose. There will be shortcomings which should be expected when taking into account design and manufacturing advances made since the last Big Healey rolled out of Abingdon into the winter sunshine of January 1968.

In general, the buyer is advised to seek the latest model type available within financial constraints, chosing an example from one end or the other of the whole price spectrum of cars available. Buy carefully, spend wisely and enjoy one of the all time great British sports cars. We shall never see their like again.

This Longbridge built BN4 was one of a batch converted to a four wheel disc brake system and fitted with twelve port head engine at Warwick. It was the 1957 Earl's Court Show Car.

3000 Mk I BN6 two seat car is similar in most visual respects to the 100-6 having common front end bodywork, radiator grille and windscreen. This car carries correct period auxiliary lamps and badge bar.

Above: *In side view the two seat versions of the six cylinder cars are very similar in appearance to the earlier 100 model series. Note how the correct specification Dunlop Road Speed tyres fill the wheel arch cut outs.*

Left: *From the rear the resemblance to the 100 is even closer. Significant differences are the smaller boot lid, external duel filler cap and pressed plinths in the shroud to carry the reflectors.*

Opposite main picture: *Although dimensionally the same as the Mk I and Mk II cars, the Mk III model assumes the appearance of a much larger car with more creature comfort.*

Opposite inset: *Despite its apparent increase in bulk, the lines of the car remain clean, smooth and beautiful with a clear line of descent from the original 100. The improved rear end ground clearance resulting from the revised exhaust system developed for the BJ8 is clearly seen in this view.*

For the Phase 3 versions of the 3000 much improved rear lamps and side turn indicators were introduced. These new lights effectively resolved the traffic problems arising from the use of a combined rear lamp, brake warning and side turn indicator within one lens. The rear view of the Big Healey has always been particularly pleasing and it is the one which most other drivers usually see!

For the 100-6, the original "100" grille badge was carried over with the simple addition of a "6" on the lightning flash. The horizontal grille bars were derived from a volume produced Austin Saloon car.

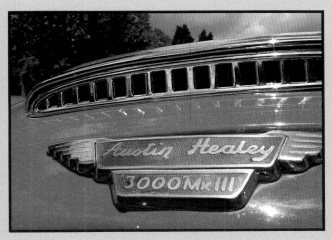

From the 3000 Convertible models onwards, front end identification was a Mark II or Mk III addition on a plinth below the Austin-Healey bonnet badge.

For the 100-6 2+2 and subsequent 3000 Mk I and Mk II models the cockpit layout followed the general theme of the "100" models, but with the rear shroud cut out extended rearwards to allow space for a pair of jump seats. The result was neat and clean without spoiling the lines of the car.

For the six cylinder cars, leather trim continued to be used for seat facings. The occasional nature of the rear seats is well illustrated here. The large door pockets were also retained.

The Mk III Convertible brought in the one and only facia style change on the Big Healey model range. The new traditional wood veneer panels and centre console imparted a Big Car feel with an aura of luxury.

The development of the Mk III brought improved rear seat access and a revision to the rear seat back to permit folding down to give a flat load floor. The hood stowage was neat, remaining in place on the car and concealed beneath an envelope bag.

The Warwick design study to develop a fixed head Coupe to extend the model range produced this 3000S model

The grille badge for the 3000S is simple and understated. Only close inspection suggests the potential behind it.

The mighty Sebring engine seen here in the 3000S Coupe and fitted with triple 2 inch SU carburettors for road use.

Also visible in this view are the reservoirs for the dual circuit twin servo brake system developed for the Sebring cars.

For the second series BN4 and BN6 models an improved twelve port cylinder head was introduced, lifting engine power output to 117 bhp. This type cylinder head was carried over onto the 3000 models and ran to the end of the production run of Big Healeys.

For the BJ8 models, the induction manifold was slightly modified over earlier models and carried twin 2 inch SU HD8 carburettors.

NAC 430F

The clean and uncluttered lines of the 3000S Coupe suggest comfort and performance, attributes which are present in abundance! Although very similar to that for the BJ8 Convertible, the windscreen on this car is slightly higher in order to further improve forward visibility.

This is the original condition, unrestored, metallic golden-beige BJ8 belonging to Dave Ramstead who contributed to the Owners View section. Only 553 cars were built in this colour. (Photo: Dave Ramstead collection).

A simple four page catalogue, Publication Number 1405 introduced the 100-6. The cover photograph is of a left hand steering car printed in reverse to give the impression of a right hand drive car for the UK market!

The 3000 Mk III Convertible catalogue was a much more comprehensive publication of eight pages in the 2035 series.

CLUBS, SPECIALISTS & BOOKS

Clubs

From the most mundane to the most exotic, almost all car marques have an associated owners club, and for the benefit of Austin-Healey enthusiasts there is a world-wide network of Clubs. In the UK, the Austin-Healey Club Ltd. is the co-ordinating body for seven autonomous club centres serving the country on a regional basis. Since the largest single market for the Austin-Healey in all its variants was the United States of America, it is not surprising that there are most clubs in that country. Because of the enormous geographical spread of the US it is impracticable for there to be one central focus, so individual clubs have been set up to serve the needs of specific areas, although many of these groups are associated in a loose connection with two national bodies,. The Austin-Healey Club of America and the Austin-Healey Club Pacific Centre. The global inter-linking of the Austin-Healey Clubs is well illustrated by the fact that the Austin-Healey Club Pacific Centre was established in 1970 as a Sub-Centre of the British Austin-Healey Club. Although now independent, a close bond remains and the Pacific Centre has grown to be the numerically largest Austin-Healey Club in the world.

The same geographical problems arise in Australia with independent Clubs serving major areas of population. There are also Clubs in New Zealand, South Africa, Continental Europe and Scandinavia, so that in almost all territories where the Austin-Healey was sold, owners have the opportunity to enjoy the benefits of membership of a club devoted to the preservation and enjoyment of a classic British sports car.

Although ownership of an Austin-Healey does not mean that membership of one of the Clubs is essential, there is much to be gained from joining the appropriate area group, since this brings the owner into contact with like minded enthusiasts with a substantial combined knowledge of the cars and the location of those sometimes difficult to find parts essential to complete or to keep a car running. There can be social benefits and introductions to specialist insurance brokers who can arrange cover on much more favourable terms than are available on the open market. There will be local area meetings and, usually, a large scale annual gathering often involving several centres or neighbouring areas. In the UK this event is International Healey Weekend; on the west coast of America there is the West Coast Meet; the Austin-Healey Club of America organises "Conclave" and on the east coast, The Austin-Healey Sports and Touring Club organise "Encounter". To attend any of these meetings is an occasion of great pleasure for the Austin-Healey enthusiast.

Britain

Austin-Healey Club GB
Mrs Carol Marks
171 Coldharbour Road
Bristol BS6 7SX
England

Australia

Austin-Healey Owners Club
94 Links Avenue Concord 2137
New South Wales

The Austin-Healey Club of Western Australia
P.O. Box 70
Maylands 6051
Western Australia

Austin-Healey Club of South Australia
P.O. Box 10
Norwood 5067
South Australia

Austin-Healey Owners Club Queensland
P.O. Box Broadway
Brisbane 4000
Queensland
Australia

Austin-Healey Owners Club Victoria
P.O. Box 105 Kew
Victoria 3101
Australia

Austin-Healey Owners Club (N.S.W.)
P.O. Box A471
Sydney South 2001
Australia

Austria

Austin-Healey Club Austria
A1220 Wien
Plankenmaistrasse 20
Austria

Super Profile

Belgium

Austin-Healey Club Belgie
Kapiteldreef 70
9831 St. Martins Latum
Belgium

Canada

Austin-Healey Owners Association of British Columbia
P.O. Box 80274
Burnaby
British Columbia V5H 3X5
Canada

Denmark

Austin-Healey Club Denmark
Viekaer 22
2950 Vedback
Denmark

France

Austin-Healey Club France
35 Quai de Grenelle
Paris 75015
France

Germany

Austin-Healey Club Germany
Leopoldstrasse 24a
D7500 Karlsruhe 1
Germany

Holland

Austin-Healey Owners Club Netherland
P. Bernhardlaan 15
2471 DV Waddinxveen
Holland

Japan

Austin-Healey Club Japan
c/o Masahiro Ishiwaka
26-3 Shibimata 5 – Chome
Katsushika – Ku
Tokyo
Japan

New Zealand

Austin-Healey Car Club New Zealand
P.O. Box 25-016
St. Heliers
Auckland
New Zealand

Austin-Healey Club New Zealand
143 Oraria Road
Johnsville
Wellington
New Zealand

South Africa

Austin-Healey Club South Africa
P.O. Box 33342
Jeppestown
South Africa

Sweden

Austin-Healey Club Sweden
Albatrosswagen 86
S136 66 Handen
Sweden

Switzerland

Austin-Healey Club Switzerland
Uberlandstrasse 199A
CH 8600 Dubendorf
Switzerland

United States of America

Austin-Healey Club of America
603 E. Euclid
Arlington Heights
Illinois 60004
USA

Austin-Healey Club Pacific Centre
P.O. Box 6197
San Jose
California 95150

Associated Regions of AHC Pacific Centre
Cascade Region
19204 64th West
Lynnwood WA98306
Bay Region
1202 Lynbrook Way
San Jose CA 95129
South-Central Coast Region
2185 Amber Drive
Woodlands Hills CA 91364
USA
Sequoia Region
775 Laurence Lane
Hanford CA 93230
Bonneville Region
1752 Paulista Way
Sandy UT 84092
USA
Rocky Mountain Region
3880 West 82nd Avenue
Westminster CO80030
USA
Arizona Region
4502 East Calle Tuberia
Phoenix AZ 85018
USA

Austin-Healey Club of Oregon
2930 Skyline Boulevard
Corvallis
Oregon 97330
USA

Austin-Healey Club of San Diego
P.O. Box 2367
San Diego
California 92112
USA

Austin-Healey Association of Southern California
P.O. Box 4082
Riverside
California 92514
USA

Austin-Healey Sports and Touring Club
P.O. Box 360
N. Baldwin
New York 11510
USA

Specialists

Throughout the production life of the Austin-Healey all franchised BMC dealers held adequate stocks of spare parts for the models and could provide competent service facilities, and this state of affairs continued for some years into the early 1970s until supplies began to taper off and dealers either folded up or switched to selling other manufacturer's products. In the lean and bleak years of the mid 1970s the only reliable source of Austin-Healey parts was the Leamington Spa business set up in 1970 by Fred Draper, previously Parts Manager for the Donald Healey Motor Company. When the Healey company decided to discontinue their spare parts operation they agreed to sell him their remaining stocks and to his establishing A-H Spares which is now the oldest specialist supplier of Austin-Healey and Jensen-Healey parts. Then in 1974 enthusiasts David Jeffrey and Laurence Mahon founded Southern Carburetters which has grown to become the world's largest manufacturer of Big Healey spares. Between them, these two companies kept Healeys on the road when interest in the marque was low, and now dominate the spare parts market in the UK as well as supplying agencies and individuals worldwide with a justified excellent reputation for quality and prompt service.

In the United States, Moss Motors of Santa Barbara, California must be the largest and probably best known supplier of spare parts for a wide range of British Sports Cars.

The gradual but steady growth of these and other emerging businesses has continued as interest in the marque has increased, to the point where most parts are fairly readily available, although certain limited demand items can still be difficult to locate. In parallel with this development there has been a growth in the number of restoration shops opening up, some good and some not so good, to handle the requirements of those owners who, for whatever reason, prefer to have their cars rebuilt by professionals. It is quite impossible to comment upon the merits of these establishments, except to say that reputations become known by word of mouth through the clubs and customers, and owners should satisfy themselves as to the competence of a businesses by personal inspection before placing work in its hands. Owners needing professional help in rebuilding or repairing their cars may consider approaching any of the businesses in the following by no means exhaustive list of service companies. Inclusion in this list should not be taken to imply any personal recommendation and exclusion should not be regarded as criticism. It is simply not possible to be aware of all the many and diverse businesses operating in this field.

Austin Healey

Specialist Parts Suppliers

SC Austin-Healey Parts
13 Cobham Way
Gatwick Road
Crawley
West Sussex RH10 2RX, England
Telephone 0293-547841/4
Formerly known as Southern Carburettors. Full, fast and efficient Spare Parts Service. Comprehensive catalogue available. World wide mail order. Mastercard and Visa accepted.

A-H Spares
Unit 7, Westfield Road,
Southern Industrial Estate
Southam
Warwickshire CV33 OJH
England.
Telephone 0962-817181
Spare parts of every description. Expert and efficient service. World wide mail order service. Visa accepted.

The Vintage and Classic Spares Company
Unit 43B Hartlebury Trading Estate
Near Kidderminster
Worcestershire
England
Telephone 0299-251353
Specialists in Lucas electrical parts of every description. Remanufactured classic headlight units now available. Mastercharge accepted.

Burlen Services
Greencroft Street, Salisbury
Wiltshire
England. Telephone 072-21777
Carburettor specialists.

M.C. Griffiths (Auto components) Ltd
13 Prince Close
North Way
Walworth Industrial Estate
Andover
Hampshire SP10 5LD
England
Telephone 0264-3650

Moss Motors Ltd
P.O. Box MG
Goleta
California 93116
United States of America
Telephone 800-235-6954 (except
California), or, 800-332-6985
(California only). The "GM" of
classic cars. Comprehensive
catalogue (AHY-04) available at a
cost of 3 Dollars. Major Credit
Cards accepted.

Hemphills Healey Haven Ltd
4-B Winters Lane
Baltimore
Maryland 21228
United States of America
Telephone 301-788-2291
Huge stocks of new and used
parts. Mastercharge and Visa
accepted.

FASPEC
1036 SE Park Street
Dept. HH
Portland
Oregon 97214
Telephone 800-547-8788 (Except
Oregon) or 503-232-1232
(Oregon only)
Specialists in British cars since
1966. Mastercard and Visa
accepted.

Sports and Classics
512 Boston Post Road
Darien
Connecticut 06820
United States of America
Telephone 203-655-8731
Specialists in British sports car
parts. Mastercharge and Visa
accepted.

A.W. Bell Nominees Pty Ltd
4-6 King Street
Oakleigh 3166
Victoria
Australia
Telephone 03-568-4622

Restoration and Repair Services

Generally the following businesses
principal activities are restoration
and repair, but in some cases a
spare parts service is also
available.

K and J.B. Restorations Ltd
The Croft
Back Lane
Long Lawford
Warwickshire
England
Telephone 078-78848
The establishment of the expert
Keith Boyer. Very competent and
detailed service covering all
aspects from full restoration to
minor repairs.

Ellis and Son Restorations
Rothersthorpe Crescent
Northampton NN4 9JD
England
Telephone 0604-61487
Although specialising in bodywork
problems, Peter Ellis can also offer
a full restoration service when
required. Friendly and efficient
service.

JME
4a Wise Terrace
Leamington Spa
Warwickshire
England
Telephone 0962-640031
Full restoration service.

Hardy Engineering
268 Kingston Road
Leatherhead
Surrey
England
Telephone 0372-378927
Gearbox and rear axle specialists.
Comprehensive range of exchange
and replacement units held in
stock. Work also carried out on
customers own units.

Healey Surgeons Inc,
7211 Carroll Avenue
Takoma Park
Maryland 20912
United States of America
Telephone 301-270-8811
Complete restoration service
backed up by comprehensive parts
catalogue. Proprietors Bruce and
Inan Phillips.

British Car Centre
Norman Nock Imported Cars Inc.
2060 N. Wilson Way
Stockton
California 95205
United States of America
Telephone 948-8767 for service
and 462-6016 for parts.
Expert restoration and service
business run by Lucas factory
trained UK expatriate Norman
Nock and his family.

Sports Cars Restored
Walter Blanck
705 Dimmeydale Deerfield
Illinois 60015
United States of America
Telephone 312-945-1360
Consultancy and spare parts
service by mail order.

Walsh Motor Works
651 E Argues Avenue
Sunnyvale
California 94086
Telephone 408-245-8502
Restoration and repair service
backed by 20 years experience.

John Chatham Cars
Bristol
Repairs, service, race car
preparation and spare parts.

Denis Welch Motors Ltd
Yoxall
Burton-on-Trent
Race car preparation and
competition parts service.

Books

The Austin-Healey had been in
production for seven years before

the first book on the marque appeared in 1960. This was "The Austin-Healey" ghosted for Donald Healey and Tommy Wisdom and it covered the then existing models from the 100, through the 100-6 to the 3000 Mk 1 and the Mk 1 Sprite. This book has been out of print for many years and is extremely rare. In the same year Pearsons published "Austin-Healey Cars" by C.P. Davidson which is a useful and concise guide to the service and maintenance of the same models.

In 1962 a book of interest to all Austin-Healey owners was published by Foulis, Written by Marcus Chambers, a former BMC Competitions Department Manager, "The Seven Year Twitch" gives a fascinating insight into the rally activities of the Big Healey in the early 1960s.

Eight years later, in 1970 "Healey and Austin-Healeys" by Peter Browning and Les Needham appeared. This was last published by Haynes-Foulis but is currently out of print.

Then in the late 1970s with the rising interest in the marque came Geoffrey Healey's definitive history of the cars entitled "Austin-Healey, the Story of the Big Healeys", followed three years later by his second volume of interest to Big Healey enthusiasts, "Healey, the Specials". These two books published by Haynes Gentry are essential reading for all Austin-Healey afficionados and tell the inside story of the conception and development of the cars.

In 1978 the prolific writer Chris Harvey produced his copiously illustrated "Healey the Handsome Brute", published by Haynes/Oxford Illustrated Press.

In 1981, Classic Car expert Graham Robson added "The Big Healeys" to MRP's Collectors Guide Series, a comprehensive and very carefully researched study of all the big Healeys.

From Motor Books International in the United States in 1984 came the "Illustrated Austin-Healey Buyers Guide" by Richard Newton. Obviously directed mainly at the U.S. enthusiast, this book provides entertaining reading and covers all models, but with the emphasis on the big cars.

Brooklands Books and "Road and Track" provide compilations of reprints of contemporary Road Test and new car descriptions. There are also two "Year Books" covering 1978 and 1979/80 containing informative chapters on the history of the cars, compiled by Paul Skilliter.

Of interest to all Austin-Healey owners will be "Sleepless Knights" by Sprite wizard John Sprinzel, published in 1962 by MRP and "More Healeys" by Geoffrey Healey which also concentrates on the Sprite models.

The most recent title dealing with the marque is "Super Profile" number F487 published by Haynes covering the original Austin-Healey 100 models.

Although some of the earlier publications have been out of print for many years, careful searching at Autojumbles and second hand bookshops can often be rewarding in building up a personal library of Austin-Healey books.

PHOTO GALLERY

1. A tranquil riverside setting for this BMC publicity photograph of a 100-6 BN6 model fitted with optional wire wheels.

2. For the BN4 and all subsequent 2 + 2 models the hood line is extended rearwards to suit the cockpit opening.

3. From the 100-6 onwards an extremely well styled Hard Top was available as an accessory.

4. The elegant and well integrated lines of the Hard Top are well illustrated in this view of a BN4.

5. For the 6-cylinder cars the grille aperture was revised to an oval shape from the shell like appearance of the 100. The horizontal grille bars are taken from an Austin A50 Saloon design.

6. For the 100-6 and most 3000 models the side marker and turn indicator functions were combined in a rather more bulbous lens than was the case for the 100.

7. For the 6-cylinder cars the folding windscreen of the 100 was deleted in favour of a fixed screen.

8. On the introduction of the six cylinder cars, the fuel filler was re-located to the top of the rear shroud close to the cockpit opening.

9. Transmission tunnel and gear lever on the 100-6 are similar to that of the BN2. The offset gearlever persisted until the introduction of the later 3000 Mk II models.

10. The central gear lever of this BJ8 has received a neat conversion to carry the overdrive switch in the knob.

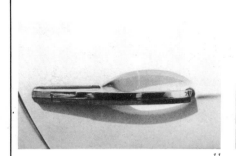

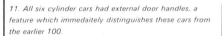

11. *All six cylinder cars had external door handles, a feature which immediately distinguishes these cars from the earlier 100.*

12. *On the 3000 Mk III models a revised push button door handle replaced the pull out handle of earlier six cylinder models.*

13. *Boot lid handle carries over from the 100 and remains unchanged throughout Big Healey model life.*

14. *Boot lid badge was a carry over from the 100 on 100-6 cars. Rear reflectors were carried on pressed plinths instead of the screw fixed pods of the 100.*

15. *All 3000 models carried an additional boot lid badge to designate engine displacement.*

16. *With the hood removed and stowed away the 100-6 cockpit has a neat appearance.*

17. *On the 3000 convertible models the hood remains fixed to the rear shroud aperture and stows beneath a clip-on envelope.*

18

19

20

21

22

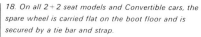

23

24

18. On all 2 + 2 seat models and Convertible cars, the spare wheel is carried flat on the boot floor and is secured by a tie bar and strap.

19. In contrast, the boot floor of the pure two seat car is unobstructed ...

20. ... the spare wheel being carried on a high platform and projects through into cockpit space behind the seats ...

21. ... as seen in this view of a BN7 cockpit.

22. For the 100-6 and 3000 Mk I and Mk II models the heating and ventilation controls are carried on a sub-panel mounted on the main facia panel.

23. A batch of 100-6 cars were fitted with four wheel disc brakes. Similar to the 100S brakes, this is the rear assembly.

24. Close up of the rear disc brake to show detail.

25

26

27

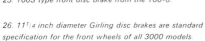

25. 100S type front disc brake from the 100-6.

26. 11¹/4 inch diameter Girling disc brakes are standard specification for the front wheels of all 3000 models.

27. All six cylinder cars have essentially the same 11 inch diameter drum brakes for the rear wheels, but for discs wheel cars the drum is modified to suit the wheel fixing studs.

28. 100-6 Chassis identification plate is carried high on the fire wall above the engine ...

29. ... whilst that for the BJ8 although similarly located is rather less accessible in the crowded engine compartment.

30. A neat dress-up accessory for the six cylinder engine is this cast aluminium rocker cover box.

28

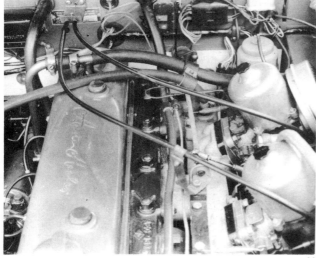

29

30

31. BN7/BT7 3000 Mk II introduced in May 1961 is distinguished from the superseded "Mk I" by a new radiator grille with vertical bars and revised bonnet lid intake aperture grille.

32. 3000 Mk III radiator grille with vertical bars carries over from the Mk II models.

33. For the third phase of Mk III production, separate side marker and turn indicator lamps were introduced.

34. Rigid framed sliding window side screens became a feature of the six cylinder cars. The large door pockets of the four cylinder cars were retained with a revised door release mechanism.

35. On Convertible models, the capacious door pockets of earlier models have to give way to the window winder mechanism.

36. Convertible cars featured a large wrap around windscreen and opening quarter lights for the doors.

31

32

33

34

35

36

37

38

39

40

41

37. There is fairly easy access to the rear seats on the Mk III 3000 when the seat backs are folded down.

38. Much care was taken over the design of the Convertible hood ...

39. ... so that it could ...

40. ... be easily ...

41. ... erected and folded by a single person.

42. The definitive 3000 Mk III Phase 3 car, twenty years after production ceased remains an impressively handsome motor car.

ERL 315D

42

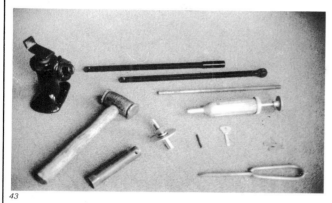

43

44

45

46

47

48

43. In comparison with the "100" tool kit, that for the 100-6 and 3000 Mk I was minimal and adequate only for very simple routine maintenance tasks. (Photo: Roger Moment)

44. Tool Kit for the BJ8 was reduced to the minimum necessary to change a road wheel. (Photo: Roger Moment)

45. BN4 100-6 2639 cc "C" series 102 bhp engine. Easy identification is possible from cast-in gallery inlet manifold with twin horizontal SU H4 carburettors.

46. BN7/BT7 3000 Mk II 132 bhp three carburettor engine.

47. Instrument layout for 100-6 and 3000 models up to Mk II follows that of the 100 but with revised graphics.

48. For the six cylinder cars the overdrive switch escutcheon plate is carried over from BN2 100.

49

50

49. Pressed steel ventilated disc wheels are standard specification for all six cylinder Big Healeys. This car is a BN7 3000 Mk I model.

50. Standard specification 3000 Mk I used in BMC publicity photograph. The cigarette connection would not be approved today!

51. BMC publicity photograph of a Mk II 3000 at Coventry airport in June 1961.

52. BN7 3000 Mk II cockpit with centre gear change lever carried over from later production BN7/BT7 models.

53. Convertible models of the Big Healey have much improved door and quarterlight seals which effectively overcame persistent water ingress problems of earlier models.

51

52

53

54

55

54. 3000 Mk I interior with Hard Top fitted (Roger Moment Collection).

55. To increase luggage carrying capacity the rear seat back on the BJ8 could be folded to provide a flat floor as seen in this publicity photograph.

56. Publicity photograph for the Swiss market. This is a Phase three BJ8 and has hexagonal hub nuts, mandatory in Swiss and certain other markets, instead of the usual "knock-off" nuts.

57. 1956 100-6 endurance records car in the Longbridge wind tunnel.

58. The streamlined high speed 100-6 in the Longbridge wind tunnel. Performance estimates based on this work proved to be remarkably accurate.

59. Abingdon Competitions Dept with works 3000 under preparation.

60. 23rd Alpine Rally, 1962. The Morley brothers in 57 ARX.

61. 23rd Alpine Rally, 1962. Don and Erle Morley on their way to a second successive victory in this event in 57 ARX.

56

57

58

59

60

61

62

63

64

65

66

62. 23rd Alpine Rally, 1962. Pat Moss, 3rd overall in 77 ARX.

63. 1963 Monte Carlo Rally. The Makinen/Carlisle car in action. Note the steel studded tyres now prohibited on open road sections. This car finished 1st in class and 3rd overall.

64. A BN7 rally car receiving attention to its triple Weber carburettor installation in the Abingdon Competition Department workshops.

65. A BJ7 on the Pavé strip at the MIRA Proving Ground. All BMC produced model types had to complete 1000 miles on this surface without major failure.

66. The 3000S fixed head coupé features a large rear window and a stylish cut off tail. Both front wings have cut out panels to help under bonnet ventilation.

67. Effortless performance is suggested by this shot of a BMC Sales Demonstration car on the move.

68. Some of the men who worked on the Big Healeys are seen here with the last of the marque shortly before it was driven off the line and exported to the United States.

67

68